LEADING A SMALL COLLEGE OR UNIVERSITY

A Conversation that Never Ends

By Harry L. Peterson

ATWOOD PUBLISHING
MADISON, WI

Leading a Small College or University: A Conversation that Never Ends
By Harry L. Peterson

© Harry L. Peterson, 2008

Atwood Publishing
Madison, WI
www.atwoodpublishing.com

Cover design by Tamara Dever, TLC Graphics, www.tlcgraphics.com
Printed in the United States of America

Note: Chapter 11 appeared in a somewhat different form in the *CASE Handbook of Institutional Advancement* (2003, 521-527).

Library of Congress Cataloging-in-Publication Data

Peterson, Harry L., 1940-
  Leading a small college or university : a conversation that never ends / by Harry L. Peterson.
    p. cm.
  Includes index.
  ISBN 978-1-891859-71-7 (pb)
  1. Small colleges—United States—Administration. 2. Universities and colleges—United States—Administration. 3. College presidents—United States. I. Title.

LB2328.32.U6P48 2008
378.1'11—dc22
                    2008013055

It is that civil conversation—tough, open, principled—between and among all members and parts of the institution that must be preserved. If it is, a community is patiently built. If it is not, the place degenerates into a center of crisis management and competing special interests. What must be open and free is the conversation between young and young, young and old, scholar and scholar, present and past—the sound of voices straining out the truth.

—A. Bartlett Giamatti
(*A Free and Ordered Space* 1989, 45)

Researchers have repeatedly found that social capital is higher in smaller settings—smaller schools, smaller towns, smaller countries, and so on. Listening and trusting are easier in smaller settings. One-on-one, face-to-face communication is more effective at building relationships and creating empathy and understanding than remote, impersonal communications.

—Putnam and Feldstein
(*Better Together: Restoring the American Community* 2003, 45–46)

ACKNOWLEDGMENTS

I learned some things during thirty-five years of university administration and leadership, which prompted me to write a book on the subject. I did not learn it all on my own, but from many others, and I want to thank them. These were good colleagues and continue to be good friends. When I am asked by friends how I like semi-retirement and whether I miss my work, I invariably say that I don't miss the work nearly as much as I miss my colleagues. Those colleagues and good friends contributed greatly to whatever success I had as an administrator and to this book.

I reported to six presidents before becoming a president myself, a long training period. I would like to thank especially Irv Shain, Bernie Cohen, Donna Shalala. and Jay Noren for the opportunity to work with them during their presidencies and chancellorships and to have learned from them. Five presidents labored through an earlier draft of this book and made very encouraging and helpful suggestions. Thank you Katharine Lyall, former President of the University of Wisconsin System; Dennis Hefner, President of SUNY–Fredonia; Michael Sheeran, President of Regis University; Ray Cross, President of SUNY–Morrisville; and my successor at Western State College of Colorado, Jay Helman, for that help.

Herbert Heneman, Emeritus Business Professor at the University of Wisconsin–Madison, reviewed my chapter on personnel decisions and made helpful suggestions. Political Science Professor Bill Niemi, of Western State College, reviewed and commented on my chapter on working with faculty.

I studied the leadership of Robert Birnbaum at the University of Wisconsin–Oshkosh while that then young chancellor made significant changes there during the mid-1970s. Bob Birnbaum met with me regularly and provided access to many of meetings at that university. It was a privilege to be able to study the presidency of an administrator who was also a student of leadership. I want to thank Bob Birnbaum for that access, as well as his later writings that helped inform much of this book.

My friend David Kindig, faculty member at the University of Wisconsin–Madison shares my fascination with what most people must surely view as the arcane subject of understanding organizations, as well as an interest in making them more effective. I thank him for his support, encouragement, friendship, and for our many conversations about this book—and many other subjects—on drives to and from trout streams.

This effort was helped enormously by support from Wisconsin Center for Advancement of Postsecondary Education at the University of Wisconsin–Madison. I want to thank Hank Lufler, Noel Radomski, and Nik Hawkins of WISCAPE for that support and help with marketing. The financial help enabled me to retain my friend and editor, Maryo Gard Ewell, who helped make this document better organized and otherwise improved it in so many ways.

I want to thank my colleagues at Western State College of Colorado, who were supportive throughout my presidency and graciously allowed me to implement my ideas for leadership at that college. There is invariably a gap between what we advise others to do in life and how we behave ourselves. I hope those colleagues will find some relationship between what I prescribe in this book and how I conducted myself as president.

This book is dedicated to two people. My late mentor, Joseph Kauffman, former college president and faculty member, was of help to me when I was his graduate student and in my administrative positions. I called upon him frequently during each of the jobs I had during my career. It was his suggestion that my book, which was then in its earliest stages, be focused on small universities. His counsel was invariably calm, wise, and thoughtful. I was a better president for his help.

My wife, Sylvia Brinkley Peterson, was a constant source of support. Her understanding of organizations, her counsel on sensitive subjects, and her exquisite understanding of the public and private contributions that a spouse can make to a presidency was unusual. That others also understood this contribution is reflected by the public acknowledgment she received throughout the time I served as president. I thank her, yet again.

HARRY L. PETERSON

TABLE OF CONTENTS

Foreword

To succeed in a job you must first understand it. My first goal in this book is to help you understand the job of president of a college or university. My second goal is to help you be successful in the job if, after you understand it, you still want to pursue it. This book is written for you.

Perhaps you are already the president of a college or university and want some tools to get a better understanding of the position in order to do a better job. This book reviews and integrates what I have found to be the most useful literature about leadership and its culture, and about organizations, as well as my own experience and that of others in actually being president. This book is written for you.

But it is not only presidents who need to know what the position is all about. People around the president, some of whom will become presidents, need to understand it, and you might be one of those people: a faculty member, department chair, dean, or vice president. Whether you decide to pursue a presidency or not, you will be able to perform your own job better and be of more help to the president and your college because you will better understand the challenges of the office. This book is written for you.

Members of governing boards can best support the president by thoroughly understanding the job. And they need a standard, a benchmark, by which to evaluate the person in that job. If you are a board member who wants to learn more about the job of your president in order to better perform your own governance role, this book is written for you as well.

Being a successful president demands intellectual skills and accumulated, technical knowledge. But it also requires, in equal measure, intuitive skills and an emotional understanding of your college or university and the people who inhabit it with you. Integrating the intellect and the emotions leads to effective leadership. While that seems to be a daunting assignment, it is one we take on every day, starting at home, as parents and spouses.

We integrate our intellect and our emotions when we listen to Johann Sebastian Bach. Although I presume there is a common experience we all have when we listen to an exceptional performance—yet, even though all of us in the audience respond as one, each of us hears Bach in a somewhat different way and at different levels of sophistication and complexity. You don't need to have taken a class in music history, studied classical music, or played a musical instrument to be touched by a Brandenburg Concerto. However, music experts, while being moved by the emotion and beauty of the sound, will also be listening for the interpretation of this particular conductor and the depth of skill of these musicians.

If you asked these experts whether they had mastered their understanding of Bach, or one of his Brandenburg Concerti, they would quickly assure you that they were still learning. They might also say that their interpretations of the composition are evolving, that they are somewhat different today than they were ten years ago. They are hearing the music through a different set of ears and a better informed brain. These experts often describe themselves as students for they can always learn more. They know this and they welcome it.

You are probably an expert in a field of study—English, history, chemistry, physics, maybe music. However, if I were to ask you a question about your field, you might quickly inform me that you do not know everything about the subject and are still learning. So it is with successful college and university presidents. They know that they have much to learn and they are always trying hard to learn more. They do it by surrounding themselves with people who know about their institution and then they listen, talk, and then listen some more to those people. They probably read, at least occasionally, books about the presidency. This book is for the students of the presidency, whether or not you will be a president, work with a president, or evaluate one.

My reading about American history and our United States presidents informs this book. When he was president of the United States, Abraham Lincoln wrote that events seemed to be controlling him, more than he was able to control events. That sentiment will be familiar to any university president. While the differences between presidents of the United States and university presidents may seem so dissimilar as to not be useful, there are compelling and fascinating comparisons. Both presidents must deal with conflicting demands and precious support from constituents as well as ambiguous goals. American presidents do not *run* the country, nor do university presidents *run* their institutions. In the best of times and circumstances they *lead*—a very different challenge. At no time are they completely in charge. Understanding that distinction can mean the difference between success and failure.

When I was writing my dissertation I gave Joe Kauffman, one of my advisors, a chapter to read and he generally approved of the content. He added, "Harry, your writing style is rather chatty and informal." It was true. I wanted it to be interesting and hoped that people would want to read it. Joe Kauffman was right, however, in seeking more formal and precise writing and I made the necessary changes.

Now, thirty-five years, a formal dissertation, and hundreds of formal memos later, I have written a book that I hope will be interesting, and that people will want to read. I hope it is, well, somewhat "chatty and informal," while still being sufficiently precise. I would like to think that Joe Kauffman would approve, and I hope you will as well.

CHAPTER 1

INTRODUCTION

Thinking about the Presidency

The test of a first rate intelligence is the ability to hold two opposed ideas in the mind at the same time, and still retain the
ability to function.

—F. Scott Fitzgerald
(*Esquire*, February 1936)

Are there as many able college executives today as in past decades?
Probably not. …The presidency is more complicated and less re-
vered than it was. In the State University field we have many able
leaders today, but they are not, I fear, the equal of those of yester-
day.

—James L. McConaughy, President, Wesleyan University, 1938
(quoted in Knight, *What College Presidents Say* 1940, 18)

The public's image of the president of a small college or university is often a romantic one. In this ideal, the president, a person of vision, is joined by scholars
and students who share that vision, and moves boldly forward with invariably
supportive trustees. The setting is bucolic, and everyone is buffered from the daily
turmoil of the world. This has not been part of my experience, nor, I suspect, has
it been yours. This romantic organization, like most ideals, probably has never existed entirely, except in our minds.

Still, it was at least partly true until the 1960s. Deference to authority has
traditionally rested on the assumption that people assigned authority deserve to
have it, but during the 1960s acceptance of, and deference to, authority were

eroded, with the Vietnam war, the civil rights movement, and the women's movement. Accompanying the erosion of authority has been a loss of social capital, the bonds that hold together communities and nations.

Deference to authority has also rested on the assumption that the authority figure possesses specialized knowledge. With the relatively recent development of the internet we can all gain access to complicated information, and decisions that may have relied on specialized information, possessed by the select few, are becoming fewer and fewer.

The democratization of information is relatively new, and its consequences will become increasingly dramatic in the years ahead. Even now, patients routinely challenge their doctors and non-credentialed reporters convey information (and misinformation) globally, instantly. The interest, indeed eagerness, in pursuing information from alternative sources is especially acute among young people who have never known any other way of conducting their lives.

University presidents in the early twenty-first century come from a generation that knew a different way of life than their students and, often, their faculty and staff. They deal daily with the consequence of the erosion of deference to authority, the democratization of knowledge which has made everyone an expert, the loss of social capital, while at the same time the competition for funding and students has increased.

If I have begun this book by making clear that leading a university is a difficult, uncertain undertaking I have accomplished my first goal. While I have identified some challenges to being successful in this job, in the chapters that follow I describe ways to respond to these challenges and greatly increase the likelihood of success.

Why do some university presidents succeed, while others fail? I know of no way to guarantee success, partly because as president you invariably do not have total control over your success or failure. However, I think I know some ways to increase the likelihood of your success. This book describes ways to make it more likely that you will be successful as a university president.

Perhaps you are a president of a college or university now. Perhaps you aspire to the job. You have devoted the last twenty or more years of effective teaching, research, and administration, to reach, finally, the capstone of your career. You want to be successful.

Your job is critical. Higher education—especially a traditional liberal arts education—has never been more important in the history of the United States. Our world requires understanding of other people and cultures, and a technologically competent and literate workforce. The need has never been greater for active and effective citizens with a grasp of local, national, and international daily news and mastery of technical skills.

While all organizations share some common characteristics, it is a central theme of this book that small colleges and universities are different in significant ways from larger ones. Understanding those differences and taking advantage of them is crucial to your success.

Those of us who spent our careers in the last half of the twentieth century often marvel that nineteenth century college and university presidents commonly taught courses in ethics and religion, as well as their academic field. How on earth did they do that?

It's not the job it was in the nineteenth century. How do you learn it? And where do you start? Steve Sample, president of the University of Southern California, relates a story from early in his administrative career. He'd just assumed a new job, and an older, respected person on the campus suggested that perhaps he was aspiring to become a university president. "Well, I don't know. I guess I've thought about it now and then," Sample said, somewhat disingenuously. The senior faculty member went on to say that he had never aspired to be an administrator, "but I've been a careful observer of ambitious men all of my life. And here, for what it's worth, is what I've learned: many men want to be president, but very few want to do president." Sample concludes: "And with that he wished me well and walked away" (Sample 2002, 202).

"Doing" president is difficult, in no small part because university presidents have the most important and difficult position at their institution, yet they typically have received the least amount of training for their position. The prestigious parts of the job, the social and professional recognition on campus and in the community, are flattering. However, what presidents do each day is hard work. And they are vulnerable, especially early in their presidencies.

THE TWENTY-FIRST CENTURY PRESIDENT

Typically, presidents, have earned doctorates in their academic fields. Graduate training is *narrow and deep*, for as knowledge has accumulated, it is impossible to be expert, or even conversant, with each area in a given field. Our studies often required isolation, increased specialization, disciplined thinking, and a methodology that broke concepts into very small pieces.

You have probably been a faculty member. Faculty work experience is also narrow and deep. Faculty typically interact with people in their discipline who mostly think as they do on important matters within and outside the university. With life experiences similar to the people we interact with every day, we tend to believe that other people see the world as we do and that those who think otherwise are at best wrong or ignorant or, at worst, badly motivated. So faculty members may have had few opportunities to deeply and regularly interact with people unlike themselves.

A university president daily interacts with many people with very different life experiences. Legislators, board members, alumni, and community members do not necessarily see the world the way the faculty do. This does not mean they are badly motivated, or want to harm your university. It does mean that their life experience and, therefore, their perspective, is different. Assuming bad motivation can result in serious problems for a university president.

As a faculty member aspiring to a presidency, you may have been chair of your academic department. You typically have served as academic deans, academic vice presidents, or provosts. In those positions you learned some things beyond your discipline and department. You learned about your institution, about management and delegation. You probably had some contact with governing boards.

But you likely have had relatively little contact with legislators, alumni, athletic departments, community members, and the media. From the *narrow and deep* world of the faculty member, you find yourself in an environment requiring *breadth*. From the academic discipline of breaking concepts into small pieces, you move into a job requiring synthesis, thinking about and understanding how the pieces are part of the whole.

You have a lot to learn. This does not mean that you cannot learn, because many college presidents have done it, sometimes with good success. This is a pretty smart group of individuals, having been leaders in teaching and research, and successful among their peers. The fact that many successfully make the transition to president is a tribute to their energy, intelligence, and perseverance. However, it is a precarious undertaking and too many do not succeed.

CHARACTERISTICS OF SUCCESSFUL PRESIDENTS

Successful presidents of small universities share an understanding of at least four things:

They understand the unique characteristics of small colleges and universities, and take advantage of that smallness. They understand their organization's culture—its history and way of doing things—which shapes the behavior of people in the university. This understanding enables them to articulate an appropriate vision, goals, and expectations of excellence. They understand what the organization needs at a particular time in its history, and they are able to focus on the organization, not on themselves.

They understand the nature of the job. Katharine Lyall, Emeritus President of the University of Wisconsin System, appointed over fifty university presidents. While most were successful, she concluded that those who failed often did so because they did not understand the job they were taking on. In this book, I try to convey something about the job, its difficulty and complexity, so you can determine whether you want to pursue a presidency. If you are already president, you may be reassured that the difficulties you are experiencing are normal and that the struggles may not be entirely of your making.

Some organizations require transformation. For instance, Ford Motors, General Motors, and United Airlines need bold leadership at this point in their history. They must drastically alter the way they do business in order to survive, and transformational leadership is essential. Toyota, on the other hand, is a model in the automotive industry. Certainly, Toyota must continue to change to meet new challenges; but a new leader determined to "transform" that company could cause it serious problems. Understanding the organization's needs at a particular time in its history and leading accordingly, makes all of the difference.

They understand people. Often, people who are important to the university behave as factions or interest groups. Faculty, governing boards, legislators, community members, and students may have unrealistic expectations of you or may resist change. As president you will be pulled in several directions at once. You may become convinced that you are the only one who understands these pressures. You may feel that you are without support.

I am convinced it is possible to identify goals that are sufficiently common, elevated, and ambitious, that the interests or factions can be united, at least most of them, most of the time. Understanding how to identify and describe those goals in a way that has meaning to diverse groups is a major challenge for a successful president.

Finally, *they understand themselves.* Successful presidents approach their jobs as students—students of the presidency—just as they saw themselves as perpetual students in their academic field. This seems simple. And yet, when consciously applied, it can change everything. You can now view challenges as puzzles to analyze and solve. You will be less apt to become intransigent and defensive, and more apt to look for more information or other points of view, or seek alternative approaches. You will engage in more thinking than acting, or at least thinking before you act.

MY PERSPECTIVE

It is customary to begin books by declaring that they were written to address a crisis. Indeed, presidential leadership has been described as "in crisis" for a long time. Commentators have decried what they believe to be increasingly short terms of presidents, and a number of presidents have received national attention because of malfeasance, conflicts with boards of trustees or faculty, and, occasionally, illegal behavior.

I am not convinced that presidential leadership is in crisis. One of the theses of this book is that the word *crisis* is over-used. During a crisis, drastic measures are too often taken without consideration of the possible consequences. Drastic measures are only occasionally appropriate.

While I don't believe there is a leadership crisis in higher education, you shouldn't be surprised when I assert that there are some significant problems. Too often, leaders fail to achieve the goals they had hoped for or that were expected of them by the board, the university, and the community when they were chosen. A detailed study of presidents in the early 1990s determined that presidents could be assigned to three categories: successful, modal, and unsuccessful (Birnbaum 1992, 89–104). Most were in the modal or average category. Significantly less than one-half were truly successful. There is an unnoticed category that the study identified: a large group of presidents who are not fired, but who plug along year after year, attending to business, but not really providing significant leadership. Their institutions drift, often getting into difficulty, slowly, over time.

I believe that some understanding of organizational theory, coupled with an understanding of the meaning of leadership accompanied by good management, can help increase the number of successful presidents and can reduce the number of average or failing presidents.

Everyone who addresses the subject of leadership does so with important underlying assumptions that inform their writing and advice. I should let the reader know my own assumptions early and clearly. I believe that the job of president is hard, and you should understand that before you pursue and assume a presidency. Yet, for all of its difficulties, I believe, as do most presidents (especially when they are not worried about the faculty or the athletic department) that it can be a good job.

A president can make a significant contribution. The work can be satisfying. I also assume that most of the people who are involved with your university—the governing board, alumni, faculty, staff, and students—want you to succeed, even though that may not always be obvious to you when you disagree with them. Do not confuse a difference in perspective or strategy on the part of the people with whom you work to a motive less lofty than your own. At its best, successfully leading a university can be a transcendent and unforgettable experience.

ORGANIZATION OF THIS BOOK

The language in the early chapters of this book is somewhat broad, theoretical, and conceptual. I found this approach to be useful as I try to convey the conceptual tools I think are necessary to understanding the organization you hope to lead. In this part of the book I may sound more like a social scientist than a former college president. Later in the book I am more specific, personal, and applied in my discussion. However, while the concepts are universal and generalizable, those ideas will be acted upon by you in your own way, just as I acted upon them as president. So, while I provide some personal examples from my time as president, you can, and should, use these ideas as best you see fit.

While this book provides some specific suggestions on how to approach the job, it is not primarily designed to be a cookbook, describing exactly the steps to take to ensure that you will be successful. Rather it treats leadership as a craft. Like other crafts, there are important principles to be understood and mastered, but the ways of implementing that understanding are yours, and depend upon your training, philosophy, and personality.

Often the terms college and university are used to differentiate two-year and four-year schools. Throughout the book I use the term universities to make it less cumbersome for the reader, as well as the writer. However, be assured, this book is designed to be helpful to presidents of both two-year colleges as well as four-year colleges and universities, which is why I included both designations in the title.

UNDERSTANDING YOUR UNIVERSITY. The first task of this book is to help you understand that your university is a complex, ambiguous, and dynamic place. It is not the job of the president to force a conceptually simple, static model on the organization, but to accept and analyze that ambiguity and complexity. Therefore, Chapter 2 discusses small universities and how they differ from large universities. Chapter 3 is devoted to organizational culture, a crucial understanding in your success, and Chapter 4 focuses on how organizations shape the behavior of faculty and staff.

UNDERSTANDING LEADERSHIP. A second task of this book is to help presidents and prospective presidents understand leadership, and how to provide leadership in a time when public mistrust of CEOs and others in authority is great. Chapter 5 addresses the sources of influence on leaders, and Chapter 6 considers the skills of effective leaders.

GETTING STARTED, AND ESSENTIAL TASKS. Finally, Chapters 7 through 12 are focused. While Chapter 7 focuses on your first year on the job, the advice in that chapter will be useful throughout your tenure. Chapter 8 describes the importance of your leadership team: whom do you want and how do you choose them? And Chapter 9 describes ways to approach faculty governance, a major problem for many presidents. Chapter 10 provides some suggestions about how you as president can work with students as a way of making your job more satisfying and understanding the other aspects of your job. Chapter 11 is devoted to external relations, an important responsibility, but one where you may have little experience. Chapter 12 provides a set of detailed suggestions on how to handle personnel searches. Only by hiring competent people who can advise you and contribute to the well being of the university will you succeed.

WHEN THINGS GO WRONG. Finally, I conclude, in Chapter 13 with a discussion of things that can go wrong during your presidency. I suggest ways of understanding and learning from them, as well as specific steps to take to recover from them.

Depending on your background, experience, and interests, you are likely to find certain chapters in the book more useful than others. I hope that the more theoretical early chapters will be useful to you, whatever your position. In those chapters I address what I believe to be universal characteristics of people in organizations.

Similarly, there are common challenges in a new, ambiguous, and challenging job, and I believe there is some useful information about how to understand and approach the crucial first year. If you are a person who likes to start in the middle to sample a book, or are very busy, you may want to start with Chapter 7, devoted to the first year. If you find it helpful you may then wish to read further.

Most of my higher education experience was in non-unionized settings, where there was a great deal of latitude in relations between administration and faculty and staff. I believe my discussion of faculty and staff governance will also be helpful for a president at a community college or a unionized institution, where relations are typically structured and hierarchical. Although I have not devoted a chapter to working with boards, it is a theme that is repeated throughout this book, and boards are treated as very important constituents. Of course, presidents in a large, public system will have less interaction with boards and probably do not report to a board directly, but to a system president or chancellor.

Personnel searches and hiring decisions are universal challenges,. I hope that the chapter devoted to searches and hiring will be useful to all readers.

While being a president will inevitably be challenging and difficult, it should be satisfying. Your job is to understand yourself and your organization and its needs at a particular time in its history. You need to create a context in which its members can thrive—where they can find meaning and do good work. And you must understand and communicate to your constituencies the meaning of what the university is trying to accomplish.

It is my hope that this book can make this important job more understandable, more satisfying, and somewhat less difficult.

CHAPTER 2

SMALL UNIVERSITIES
Why Are They So Special?

Daniel Webster, who later became one of the most respected U.S. Senators of the nineteenth century, argued the right to independence of Dartmouth College, opposing New Hampshire statutes that placed it under state control.

Webster declared to the judge, "Sir, you may destroy this institution. It is weak; it is in your hands! I know it is one of the lesser lights in the literary horizon of our country. You may put it out. However, if you do, you must carry through your work! You must extinguish, one after another, all those greater lights of science which, for more than century, have thrown their radiance over our land!

"It is, sir, as I have said, a small college. And yet there are those who love it."

Joseph Story, the justice in the case, wrote, "the whole audience had been wrought up to the highest excitement; many were dissolved in tears." When Webster prevailed in the case, "the students celebrated by firing a cannon." The grateful college arranged for Gilbert Stuart to paint Webster's portrait, which today hangs in Dartmouth's Webster Hall

(from Peterson, *The Great Triumvirate: Webster,*
Clay and Calhoun 1987, 101).

The first chapter of this book provided a brief overview of some of the challenges facing higher education in general, and its leadership in particular. The last chapters of this book explore specific challenges in you will face as president. But addressing specific situations can only be done effectively after understanding the context of some important ideas about organizations and leadership. I start by looking at organizations.

MODELS FOR UNDERSTANDING UNIVERSITIES

Modern organizations are complex and universities are perhaps the most complex of all. To lead a university, you must understand it as an organization. You need analytical tools to make sense of what you are observing and experiencing in the university. This is especially true if you are moving from one type of organization to another.

Robert Birnbaum has developed four conceptual organizational models of universities. He writes: "A model serves as a conceptual lens that focuses our attention on some particular organizational dimensions; but in the process of doing so it inevitably obscures or obliterates other dimensions. Models create perceptual frames or 'windows on the world'" (1988, 83). Here, I review all four of these models.

The Bureaucratic Institution

This type of organization emphasizes reporting lines and detailed position descriptions. The focus is on formal authority and communication. The organization is *tall*, meaning that there are many layers of authority. Most of the information the president receives about the organization is from the people who have formal reporting relationships to the president. Emphasis is on rationality and clear divisions of labor. Public community colleges are most likely to be bureaucratic institutions.

The Anarchical Institution

This type of organization is large and decentralized. The parts of the organization are loosely coupled, and people are primarily oriented to their immediate colleagues and their academic fields. The organizational goals are many and vague and the decision-making is unclear. There is no over-arching statement of purpose for the university, or if there is, it does not provide an immediate reference or form of guidance for the university members. The evolution of the academic program is not undertaken in a systematic, orderly, and sequential way, but evolves very informally over time, typically in response to changes in academic areas that take place outside the organization. The organizational culture relies heavily on "national meritocractic standards based on the professional and expert authority of the faculty" (Birnbaum 1988, 153). Large research universities are most likely to be anarchical institutions.

The Political Institution

This type of university is composed of subgroups whose members strongly identify with other members of their group. The identification may be around academic departments, but is often organized around other factors such as age, gender, ethnicity, or ideology. The organization may have undergone significant changes, reflected in the types of groups on campus such as older faculty members, newer arrivals, faculty with doctorates, and "old timers" who may not have doctorates. Power is diffused among various groups who may or may not ally with one another to achieve their desired ends. While there is broad agreement on the campus about the goals of the institution, members of each group typically believe that their program is the most important. Authority is dispersed so that no one group can dominate others on campus; this creates stability. There is competition for limited funds. Factions put political pressure on one another and on the administration. The president acknowledges and understands these pressures, considers them, and works with the various groups to advance the presidential agenda. Large, comprehensive, state universities with a strong faculty union typify political institutions.

The Collegial Institution

Hierarchy is not as important at this type of institution, and the college is egalitarian and democratic. The faculty sees their president, not as an independent authority, but as their agent whose authority stems largely from their support. The faculty expects to be regularly consulted. The ties among the faculty and between the faculty and the administration are informal and the interaction is constant. "Collegial members interact and influence each other through a network of continuous personal exchanges based on social attraction, value consensus, and reciprocity" (Birnbaum 1988, 95). The organizational culture at such a university tends to honor the past, strongly influences the behavior of people within the organization, and is widely agreed upon. Small private colleges or universities are most likely to be collegial institutions. As Birnbaum writes:

> No model of a complex system such as a college or university can be a perfect representation of that system, but some models appear to reflect what usually happens in some parts of some institutions and therefore suggest useful courses of action. (1988, 83)

A Collegial and Political University

I have included all four of Birnbaum's models in order to help you to consider the key elements that characterize the institution that you lead, or hope to lead. This is not to suggest that you are likely to have the skills to adapt your leadership style to be successful in very different types of institutions. We cannot morph into someone we are *not*; but we can work within our set of skills and personality to make the most of who we *are*. Two of the four models, the collegial and the political, are especially applicable to small public and private colleges and universities. The applicability of the collegial model is obvious and is consistent with the entire focus of this book. The political model is useful to some degree in understanding any type of university. Universities of all sizes have groups of constituents who believe that their interests and programs are of paramount importance. Academic departments, groupings of departments, external constituents like businesses or accrediting bodies, board members, students and student groups, alumni, athletics, parents—all want their interests satisfied, and place pressure on the university accordingly, requiring political skills on the part of the president to mediate those pressures, which I discuss further in Chapter 6.

Birnbaum was considering a mythical, prototypical, private college when he described the collegial model. But the model is generally applicable to small public colleges or universities. Still, there are constraints, for example, small public universities in large state systems of higher education, which receive their funding through system allocations, that are constrained by the rules of that system and legislative mandates. Just as "small" does not automatically mean "collegial," neither does "private." Because these are pure conceptual models, it is best to think of them as tools which, when applied to a specific university are, necessarily, an imperfect fit. The goal is not to force the institution into such a model, but to consider your university and use the model to gain insights into its operation. While the collegial model is the most important of the four models for the purposes of this book, the political model is also helpful.

Descriptive Characteristics of a Collegial University

A president or prospective president can use Birnbaum's models to help determine an effective leadership strategy. Before you consider leadership, however, it is essential to have an understanding of your organization. How do you identify a "collegial" university?

Schuman suggests that a college with 500 to 3,000 students qualifies as being small, although he acknowledges that this range is somewhat arbitrary (Schuman 2005, 46). I believe these numbers are useful, but that for the purposes of this book, the number of students can be greater. As the number of students increase, and the number of faculty and staff increase, the ability to lead in a way suggested in this book diminishes somewhat. For this reason, it is helpful to think of size along a continuum rather than an absolute number.

This book emphasizes that small colleges and universities are different. It is, in fact, size that makes more likely the presence of certain characteristics. Birnbaum suggests that "Collegiality, seen as a community of individuals with shared interests, can probably be maintained only where regular face-to-face contact provides the necessary coordinating mechanisms and where programs and traditions are integrated enough to permit the development of a coherent culture. Size is probably thus a necessary but not sufficient condition of a collegium, and this limits the possibility of the development of collegiality on an institutional level to relatively small campuses" (Birnbaum 1988, 93). If a given characteristic is not present, the president may have the potential to develop it to the university's advantage. The list includes:

- Face-to-face interaction among faculty, typically across academic departments.
- High levels of agreement among faculty, staff, and administration about the mission of the university.
- High degree of informality among faculty, staff, administration, and students.
- Presidential authority conferred in large part by the faculty who were involved in making the choice of leadership.
- Agreement among parties important to the university such as faculty, staff, students, alumni, and administration—on symbols important to the university and its history.

- Reduced social distance between the leader and the faculty, compared to other universities.

- Communication moving not only from the top down, but from the bottom up, and across organizational units.

You must analyze the extent to which they are true for your institution. It is helpful to think of them as being on a continuum, not one or the other. There are special characteristics of successful small universities that a president must recognize in order to be effective—they are not simply miniature versions of larger universities, although they are too often treated as though they are. Also, there can be external constraints on the collegiality of small universities. For example, unions in an institution within a state system can affect the collegiality of a small public university. Unions tend to formalize relationships and systems, while they provide helpful stability and protection of resources, can impose strains that limit the possibilities for collegiality.

CONTRASTING LARGE AND SMALL UNIVERSITIES

Let us consider some of the more obvious contrasts in the nature of the job.

From the early to the mid-twentieth century, the name of a large, visible university was often synonymous with the name of its president. At the University of Chicago, it was Robert Hutchins from 1929–1951. At Notre Dame, Father Theodore Hesburgh in the 1960s. (Indeed, when people thought of Notre Dame, they thought of Father Hesburgh, on occasion, even before the football team.) At the University of Wisconsin, Charles Van Hise in the early twentieth century. For the University of California System, it was Clark Kerr in the 1960s.

Today, people typically identify these universities by their noteworthy academic fields. They count the number of members of the National Academy of Science or Nobel Prize winners. Presidents of such institutions spend most of their time doing external work: raising funds, working with governing boards, defending and explaining the university to alumni and, at public universities, legislators and governors. People decry the decline in the quality of leadership in these large, prestigious universities, when in fact, the opportunities to lead have declined. Except under special circumstances—when the university is threatened or in crisis, for instance—the most successful of these university presidents are remembered for beginning or enhancing a few academic programs or raising funds for buildings, typically from alumni. The greatly reduced deference to authority, as well as the numerous and diverse constituencies that drive the life on large universities today, do not allow for the kind of leadership that was present in earlier times. It does not mean that the presidents of these universities are any less talented or dedicated.

The presidency of the small university is quite different. The president can still be an important figure to the board, faculty, and alumni who look to the person in that office to help define the goals of the institution and to articulate those goals inside and outside of the university. If students think about such things (which they do irregularly), they too look to the president for leadership. Personality and leadership matter, and formal presidential authority for policies and practices in a small university, as assigned by its governing board, is often greater than in a large university.

The failure to recognize the uniqueness of smallness means missing important opportunities for leadership. Let me describe several of the most important and suggestive realities of small universities. While organizations of all sizes are affected by their environment, which shapes their history, their resources, and their politics, small universities (excepting those few selective colleges with very large endowments) are typically more vulnerable to external influence. There are fewer people inside and outside the organization to convince of the soundness of a given change, and communication is less complex. At the same time, partly because of their smallness, they can respond to those forces—including changes in the competitive marketplace—more quickly and strategically than can a larger institution. With effective leadership, small organizations can be nimble, which is crucial in the twenty-first century.

Small colleges and universities must be focused in undertaking new activities. In the corporate world, Wal-Mart daily adds and drops products and the 3M® Corporation regularly creates new products, but both maintain a consistent corporate identity. The same is true for large universities, which add and drop activities while remaining recognizable. In small institutions, successful leaders recognize where the potential for excellence lies; but for their institution to excel in these areas, the president must make crucial choices, possibly discontinuing existing programs for the sake of a new program. Clear and precise missions, core values, and goals are essential if these choices are to be made without sacrificing the institution's character.

A significant concern of most small universities is the availability of resources. Large research universities attract millions of dollars in support from the federal government, as well as from private sources, especially alumni who are typically interested in supporting their own field of study. This money provides training support for graduate programs and equipment, both of which help fund undergraduate education. By contrast, smaller public universities are typically heavily dependent on state tax dollars and tuition which provide relatively little money for innovation and new or experimental programming. Yet, at smaller universities, private gifts, even relatively small private gifts, can have a dramatic and immediate impact. While there are fewer potential large donors, they are more likely to identify with the university as a whole, so they are likely to be more receptive to a broader use of their contribution.

In a small university, leaders, faculty, and staff are more able to see and understand the whole institution. They are more apt to understand their stake in the entire organization than are faculty and staff in a larger university. This makes it less difficult to develop institutional goals, to communicate those goals, and to implement change. Also, smaller organizations tend to generate a greater emotional bond and deeper loyalty than do large organizations. In part this is because of the face-to-face relationships that characterize small places. Because faculty members often lack national reputations, large research grants, or direct teams of graduate students, they also lack the financial autonomy or job prospects that might prompt them to identify more with colleagues in their discipline outside their university and greater internal loyalty results. Finally, the vulnerability of a small university often leads to a greater sense of responsibility to provide support among all of its members.

In large organizations, faculty and staff tend to interact as members of groups with similar interests. At Harvard University, for example, confidence or lack of confidence in president Lawrence Summers was related to departmental affiliation: the letters and sciences faculty were mostly opposed, while the law and the professional school faculties were mostly supportive. It is doubtful that many of those faculty talked with faculty in opposing groups. Faculty form political coalitions based on common interests, temporary and long-standing. Their conflicts about issues such as allocation of funding are typically ideological. In small universities, conflict is more likely to be individual and personal and involve an added emotional dimension—after all, the people involved may need to interact with one another the next day. In small universities, the direct relationships presidents form with faculty and staff introduce a personal element into the mix that is often not true in larger places.

In a large organization, the changes a president can make are often tied to specific programs or occur at the margins. Although organizations of any size tend to continue to do what they have always done, changing the status quo in a large place is a massive, and often daunting, undertaking. By contrast, at a small university, both internal and external constituencies are more apt to look to the president for direction and significant changes can be associated with this individual's leadership. These organizational characteristics can make the position of president at a small university attractive, for the potential for impact is greater. Still, if the president cannot lead, or makes unwise choices with precious, limited resources, the college is more vulnerable. Influence, or the exercise of authority, is neutral by itself. It can be used for good or ill.

It is important to understand the broad context of your university, and I believe these typologies are useful for that purpose. However, you also need tools to understand the idiosyncratic nature of your institution, its history and culture. Without that understanding failure is guaranteed. In the next chapter we examine organizational culture.

CHAPTER 3

ORGANIZATIONAL CULTURE

How to Make Sense of Your University

We need myths to get by. We need story, otherwise the tremendous randomness of experience overwhelms us. Story is what penetrates.

—Robert Coover
(quoted by Garrison Keillor on *The Writer's Almanac* 2004)

The past is never dead. It's not even past.
—William Faulkner
Requiem for a Nun (Act I, Scene III)

When boards and colleges are searching for a new president they place ads in the *Chronicle of Higher Education*. They briefly, typically glowingly, describe the history of their university, its size, budget, and the ambitious, indeed impossible, set of characteristics they are seeking in a new president. Their secret or not so secret goal is to find someone very much like the previous president, if that individual was successful. More often, they are looking for strengths that the previous president did not possess.

While all subjects are important and helpful in finding a competent leader who is a good fit for the university, the ads usually leave out some of the most important questions. Effective search committees should have some reasonable agreement on the story that people involved with the university tell themselves and others when asked about the school. It is that story that causes people to work together when they go to work each day.

Only after I began my job as president of Western State College did I learn that the college had lost its authority to offer graduate programs about ten years before my arrival, a loss still deeply felt by those on campus and in the community. When I went to the post office in Gunnison on one of my first days on the job, the postal clerk asked me, "Well, are you going to get the graduate program back?" I made a casual joke about it when I made my first annual address to the faculty and staff in the fall. Although the reception to my remarks was pretty well received, the comment by the postal clerk was one that I learned to take seriously. The loss of the graduate program symbolized to the college and community the rapid turnover in presidents, the lack of continuity of leadership, the lack of strong leadership, and a governing board that they believed had not represented their interests. Five years later, when I was invited to testify before a committee reviewing public higher education in Colorado, I affirmed the need to return the authority to offer graduate programs at Western State College.

A president's effective leadership requires an understanding of what motivates the organization's people and shapes their behavior. Successful presidents, especially intuitive presidents, learn some of these things as their careers progress. Failing to understand their organization's culture causes many presidents to founder. The previous chapter was mostly descriptive: In it, I described the characteristics of a small university, and I suggested the collegial model as the best way to understand your organization. This chapter provides some tools for you to understand the important forces in your university—an understanding that leads to getting things accomplished. This chapter and the next draw on research about the effects of organizations and other social settings on individual behavior.

In Chapter 1, I observed that presidents typically come to their job with narrow academic specialization, followed by traditionally bureaucratic administrative work. They may be comfortable with organizational charts, position descriptions, and reporting lines. This knowledge is essential for the job, but, by itself, very inadequate for effective leadership. There are powerful forces at work in an organization which will overwhelm your efforts to lead—especially your efforts to bring about significant change—if you do not understand and work with them.

All organizations share certain characteristics. They all have goals, they produce goods or provide services, and they have members. The people in the organization have different assignments and are organized in a way to accomplish those goals. Some people have authority over other people. All this is true in higher education. However, the individual autonomy and collective authority of the faculty, as well as the loose connections of the work units, create a degree of decentralization that is unusual and which pose leadership challenges.

WHAT IS ORGANIZATIONAL CULTURE?

The United States government keeps demonstrating that helping people in other countries write a constitution that provides opportunities for citizens to choose their leaders is not a sufficient condition for democracy. A nation's people must develop a tradition of voting as a way of expressing views and choosing leaders, and accepting the results even when many voters disagree with them. When Alexis de Tocqueville visited our country in the 1830s he marveled at the way that Americans conformed to a set of unwritten rules that made it possible for our young country to be governed democratically. Tocqueville called these the *habits of the heart*, and they defined a strong culture of democracy.

Just as countries, communities, tribes, and ethnic groups have habits, passing from generation to generation, so do organizations. Over time, organizations establish certain ways of accomplishing their goals, of doing their business. These established patterns become deeply embedded in the organization and define how members do things. This is true of routine ways of performing tasks. It is especially true when large and important goals of the organizations are at stake.

When college presidents make decisions and issue instructions for these decisions to be implemented, they are sometimes enormously frustrated to find that their order was not followed. Often that is because their directive violates the culture of the university. Understanding and working within the culture—the "habits"—is among your major responsibilities. Changes that call on that culture and are explained as fitting within it are most likely to be successful and to persist beyond your presidency. Such a skill takes imagination, intuition, creativity, and careful listening. (More about that in Chapter 7, which discusses assuming the presidency and the crucial first year on the job.)

Often university presidents view organizational culture as a manifestation of stubbornness and rigidity, an obstacle to change. I know a president who, in a moment of deep frustration, said that it would be a lot easier to accomplish things if her university were new and without *any* history. But if you are to be successful in changing the way your college goes about its work or in altering its goals, you must first learn how your new institution does things. By knowing this, and working within the organization's culture, you can effect change.

The importance of organizational culture cannot be overstated. Consider the merger of two organizations or the acquisition of one organization by another. Most mergers fail, never achieving the goals of increased productivity or efficiency. The most frequent reason for this failure is that the cultures of the two organizations are not compatible and cannot be effectively blended (Kanter 1989). If cultures are strong and enduring in organizations that make tangible, recognizable products, consider how strong must be the values and ways of doing things in venerable organizations whose "product" includes a belief system and a body of knowledge. Examples include churches, military organizations and, of course, colleges and universities.

Members of such organizations believe strongly that adhering to important parts of their history, imparting the story of that history to its new members, and continuing it into the future is an important responsibility. They exert powerful socializing effects on their new members who must adhere to these values and traditions in order to succeed. They may even confuse its core beliefs, important to retain and perpetuate, with day-to-day tasks and ways of accomplishing its goals, and may resist even unimportant changes.

THE POWER
OF ORGANIZATIONAL CULTURE

A classic article from the 1940s by sociologist Robert Merton, "Bureaucratic Structure and Personality," addresses some of these problems. Merton writes that people in organizations develop a "trained incapacity" to change and to deal with new challenges. They keep on doing what they have been doing, whether it works or not. It may have worked at one time and it is comfortable for the organization's members, but the behavior now has a life of its own. It is no longer a means to an end.

Merton writes: "Trained incapacity refers to that state of affairs in which one's abilities function as inadequacies or blind spots. Actions based upon training and skills which have been successfully applied in the past may result in inappropriate response *under changed conditions*" (Merton 1957, 198). I am reminded of Harvard psychologist Gordon Allport's description of motives for human behavior becoming "functionally autonomous." The neurotic symptoms remain, although the reasons for their existence do not (Allport 1937).

Organizations that have developed a culture that is not responsive, that resists new ideas and challenges, are vulnerable. The worst examples tend to be large, hierarchical organizations without competition that recruit leaders heavily from within, and serve a clientele neither able to go elsewhere for service, nor to complain effectively. These are reasons why the Bureau of Indian Affairs and the Immigration and Naturalization Services are probably the two most inept and unresponsive federal agencies.

Not only can organizations effectively resist change, and resist the ideas of new leadership, but they can also reject the leaders themselves. The *New York Times*, arguably the best newspaper in the United States, attracts outstanding reporters, treats them with respect, and provides them with a high degree of professional autonomy. The publisher of the *New York Times* named an editor who was autocratic and dictatorial, who violated the historic organizational culture of that newspaper. He lasted about two years in the job: the staff rebelled against the way he treated them and caused him to be fired.

Here are a few examples of how organizational cultures can facilitate or inhibit change and accomplish basic goals. They are of organizations that have rather different missions: the Central Intelligence Agency, the Federal Bureau of Investigation, the American automobile industry, the Roman Catholic Church, and NASA. You may know some or all of these stories, none of which, intentionally, is from the world of higher education. It is often easier to see parallels if the specifics are not too familiar, seeing things more clearly in organizations that we are not so close to.

Consider the CIA and the FBI. The CIA must perform much of its work in secret; but it has built upon that secrecy to a degree that it has become unaccountable and dysfunctional. The CIA and its career civil servants keep information from one another; they do not share information with other branches of government. They keep right on doing what they have done for years. Directors of the CIA come and go. They are sometimes brilliant, but at least bright and dedicated individuals who work to make the CIA responsive to the needs of the country. The directors of the agency work hard to make changes, yet, in spite of their best efforts, the CIA keeps right on doing what it has done for the last forty years. Included in this behavior is the failure to cooperate with the FBI, even though their goals are complementary.

The FBI's history of early success helped create a mystique of invulnerability, resulting in an unusual degree of autonomy for a federal agency. This autonomy has evolved into insularity which makes the FBI unable to respond to the requirements of the twenty-first century. A book written after the 9/11 attacks describes a meeting of a staff member of the National Security Council and two FBI officials at the White House. "The NSC man was excited and surprised to learn from some old press clippings that Ayman al-Zawahiri, the much-feared Egyptian terrorist and deputy to Osama bin Laden, had visited the United States on a fundraising trip in the early 1990s. 'I couldn't believe it,' he explained to the FBI men. 'Did you know that?' The two gumshoes nodded warily. 'Well,' the staffer continued, 'if he was here, someone was handling his travel and arranging his meetings and someone was giving him money. Do you know who these people are? Do you have them covered? There are cells here and we need to know about them.' 'Yeah, yeah, we know. Don't worry about it,' the FBI officials replied" (Thomas 2002).

Two organizations crucial to national security; two organizational cultures that prevent them from interacting, even when stakes are unthinkably high. Their important needs for secrecy in conducting their work enabled them to cover up their mistakes and prevented them from sharing information with one another. The problem is so serious that the late Senator Daniel Patrick Moynihan, an expert on intelligence matters, recommended well before the terrorist attacks, that parts of the intelligence community simply be abolished and new agencies created.

Another example: The American automobile industry began losing market share to the German and Japanese automakers in the 1960s. Compared to their competitors overseas, the quality of American cars was poor. Although the quality has improved substantially, American cars continue to be less reliable than Japanese cars. The American automotive industry had developed an organizational culture of mediocrity, with little concern for the customers or the competition. General Motors, the least responsive of the Big Three manufacturers, tried to break away from its historical organizational culture when it developed the Saturn, building that plant in Tennessee, away from all of their other divisions, using as many new staff and workers as possible. They hoped, in this way, to emulate their competitors. They have been only partially successful.

The Roman Catholic Church is an organization that prides itself on its history and tradition. Because its belief system includes veneration of the past, change is especially difficult. Most problematic, from the point of view of Church reformers, is that all of the leadership of the Church comes from the inside, after many years of socialization in the ways of the Church. Would Pope John XXIII have been selected as Pope in the late 1950s if the Cardinals doing the selecting had known of the changes he would introduce?

The Catholic Church is one of the largest, oldest, and most bureaucratic organizations in the world. It provides direction and moral leadership to millions of followers throughout the world. Yet, when priests exploited their authority by sexually abusing children in their parish, the Church hierarchical response has been to protect its priests, not to correct obvious and grievous wrongdoing to the people it serves. An organization whose purpose is providing moral direction to its millions of members could not apply its teaching to itself. The result has been payments to victims of over $1 billion

The National Aeronautics and Space Administration, NASA, was created in the early 1960s to develop the American space program and put a man on the moon before the end of the decade. It was one of the most spectacular governmental success stories of the twentieth century. NASA attracted the best and brightest engineers, scientists, and pilots. But by the early twenty-first century it had become unable to respond to new challenges, sloppy about quality, and protective of its employees. In a relatively short period of time it had gone from one of the most innovative and responsive government agencies to being bureaucratic and defensive. While the problems resulting in the Challenger tragedy were described as "technical," the cause of the technical problems was a stagnant organization whose members did not communicate and respond.

On the other hand, organizational cultures can be extremely positive forces. The culture can embrace important goals. It can value innovation. It can maintain high standards. Organizations with strong, effective cultures attract talented people, retain the best of those people, and shape their behavior. An organization can be old and large, with an organizational culture that perpetuates a standard of excellence. The U.S. Marine Corps is over 225 years old. Early in its history it established a reputation of attracting some of the best military volunteers. Its leadership is chosen from within its ranks, and while turnover is a reality, especially among the lower ranks, it continues to attract dedicated recruits who embrace that mission and perpetuate it because of its strong history of leadership and its clear mission.

Another example comes from the health care industry in the United States, where one of the major challenges is containing costs. Health Maintenance Organizations, or HMOs, have been created to help address that problem. Although they have at least partially succeeded in containing costs, HMOs have struggled to gain acceptance, both by the people who work for them and by the people they serve. Physicians are typically trained to be private practitioners and patients want to choose their physician. And yet Kaiser Permanente, an HMO that began in California in the 1930s, has a reputation for providing excellent health care and its physicians and staff accept its way of doing business. Kaiser Permanente attracts high quality health care professionals who function well in that large bureaucracy; its patients express a high degree of satisfaction with their care. Kaiser's professionals and patients alike knowingly join a prestigious organization that works well. However, when Kaiser expanded its program beyond California to other states it failed. The *New York Times* reported, "Kaiser often tried to move quickly by contracting with individual practitioners instead of sticking with its model of Kaiser doctors working in Kaiser Clinics. 'To the extent that we tried to be something we're not, we failed,' said George Halvorson, Kaiser's chief executive" (Kohr 2004).

Many individuals have led the seven organizations I have just described. Leaders came and went; only a few are remembered. Some of them were effective and understood the culture of their organization and worked within that culture. Others failed. The organization, shaped by its culture and the understanding of the organization by its leader, was a crucial factor in that success or failure.

ORGANIZATIONAL CULTURE IN HIGHER EDUCATION

The most important writing on the subject of organizational cultures in higher education is *The Distinctive College*, by sociologist Burton Clark. He wrote almost forty years ago about old, small, elite, liberal arts colleges. He described "organizational sagas" at Antioch, Reed, and Swarthmore (Clark 1970). Clark writes: "organizational saga refers to a unified set of publicly expressed beliefs about the formal group that (a) is rooted in history, (b) claims unique accomplishment, and (c) is held with sentiment by the group" (Clark 1972).

Rice and Austin, writing about small, successful colleges say, "These are colleges with strong, penetrating cultures. They share with most other liberal arts colleges several intrinsic advantages that strengthen culture: their relatively small size, interdependent parts, and a long history—they have traditions on which to build. What is special about these cultures, however, is their coherence. They say what they do, in very clear terms—then do what they say. A coherent culture permeates the fabric of an institution; you hear the same stories—the college lore—whether talking to the chairman of the board, a mathematics professor, a freshman, or the campus police" (Rice and Austin 1988, 52).

These stories—sagas—describe accomplishments of the institution. They become mythical in nature, they become simpler in the telling and they invariably have a moral. They are embraced over the years by the faculty, the administrators, board members, and students. Students, of course, become alumni, important sources of support and influence for universities. Only presidents who understand the symbols arising from these sagas will lead successfully.

While Clark was writing about highly selective organizations with ample re-sources which, therefore, are more protected from their external environment than most small universities, every college and university has a saga. It may not be as distinctive or as compelling, but it is a collective understanding by the members of the organization about their organization and its history. It shapes the behavior of the people in the organization. Clark observes that in other, less prestigious, organizations, "Even when weak, the belief can compensate in part for the loss of meaning in much modern work, giving some drama and some cultural identify to one's otherwise entirely instrumental efforts" (Clark 1972).

The stories that organizations tell about themselves, like stories told by families, ethnic groups, and countries, are partly rooted in fact; but they have a life beyond those facts. One does not need to be a social scientist to understand this. A cartoon in *The New Yorker* magazine depicts a group of young boys, camping, gathered around a fire, assuming a seriousness beyond their years. One boy says, "Someday, when we're old, we're going to look back and embellish this" (*The New Yorker*, September 1, 2003).

It is allegiance to these organizations and common cultural experiences that result in deep affection, not just on the part of today's employees, but also on the part of alumni. And this affection prompts large donations of private support. While the affection for a large university can be intense, the relationships between students, faculty, and staff, and the connection to the institution is generally more easily established at a smaller university.

An organization's leader, then, can reinforce or shape the organizational saga and generate commitment to that organization. Presidents must learn this saga, this culture. They must enter it carefully and make changes consistent with it if they are to be successful. The saga can facilitate change. It can suggest to you frameworks for action, ways in which you can lead your institution towards change, towards becoming the engines of social and economic mobility that they can be. Yet sagas can also be used by groups—often the faculty—to justify their unwillingness to change, to resist outside pressures, perhaps invoking a venerable tradition, such as academic freedom. And indeed, resistance to outside pressures may account for much of the historical success of the university. One of your challenges, then, is to recognize when "saga" can be an ally in moving an institution forward, and when it is a force for stagnation.

Understanding your organization's culture is a crucial first step. But you must also understand how individuals and groups behave within the framework of a culture if you are to provide effective leadership.

How Organizations Shape Our Behavior

Why Do People Do the Things They Do?

Part of the folly of our time is the idea that we can see the whole
of something by looking at the pieces, one at a time.

—Ben Logan
(*The Land Remembers* 2006, 3)

Our Need for Meaning

Having talked in general terms about organizational culture, I turn to examining
its impact on individual behavior. Residential communities—neighborhoods—
can be powerful shapers of human behavior. Eric Klinenberg's *Heat Wave* tells the
story of a terrible hot week in Chicago in 1995 that took hundreds of lives.
Klinenberg compares two seemingly similar communities, Little Village and
North Lawndale, both with large numbers of poor and elderly people. Yet, when
faced with a crisis, people in the two neighborhoods behaved quite differently.

In Little Village, predominantly Hispanic, the fatality rate was low. People
knew one another and residents checked on neighbors who might need help.
There was a rich network of interpersonal relationships and support. In contrast,
in North Lawndale, predominantly African American, the fatality rate was high.
Isolation, fear, and dysfunction prevailed. The culture of each community literally meant the difference between life and death.

North Lawndale had ten times the fatality rate of Little Village. Why? Because Little Village is a bustling, relatively safe, close-knit Hispanic community;
the elderly had family and friends nearby who could look in on them and streets

and stores where they could go to escape their stifling apartments. North Lawndale, by contrast, is a sprawling, under-populated, drug-infested neighborhood. The elderly there were afraid to go outside and had no one close by to visit them.

The heat was deadly only in combination with particular social and physical circumstances (Gladwell 2002).

The importance of residential communities is obvious to most of us. Yet residential communities are less close-knit than they have been, in part because Americans live farther and farther from where they work, work longer hours than in any other country in the world, and spend less time at home. Furthermore, extended families, many with historic ethnic and racial roots, are now more often scattered throughout the country, decreasing the amount of time that family members spend with one another. Attendance at church and at other social institutions has been declining. Even private or family experiences are less likely to be able to be shared outside the family: with the proliferation of magazines, the internet, television, and home movie theaters, fewer people share a common experience. During the 1950s we were a nation that tuned in together to *I Love Lucy* and the *Ed Sullivan Show*. Today, we are more likely to sit at home, logging onto the Internet, while the kids play computer games, frequently alone. Robert Putnam, whose work is discussed later in this chapter, comments: "

> The distinctive effect of technology has been to enable us to get entertainment and information while remaining entirely alone. That is from many points of view very efficient. I also think it's fundamentally bad because the lack of social contact, the social isolation means that we don't share information and values and outlook that we should. (Putnam 2006, A18)

A study by sociologists at Duke University and the University of Arizona concluded that "most adults only have two people they can talk to about the most important subjects in their lives—serious health problems, for example, or issues like who will care for their children should they die. And about one-quarter have no close confidants at all" (Fountain 2006).

Opportunities for Americans to feel they are a part of something larger than themselves have been diminishing. Yet our needs for one another and for community remain. Work communities evolved as the places for relationships, support, and meaning. But workplaces themselves are changing, as are products and services, to accommodate a fast-paced, world economy. Once again, meaning decreases. But as Clark noted almost forty years ago, even weak organizational sagas "can compensate, in part, for the loss of meaning in much modern work" (Clark 1972, 179).

SMALL GROUP BEHAVIOR

Within your college are countless small groups. Students form friendships with their roommates or with others of similar academic or social interests. Faculty and staff work in departments or other work units, typically performing tasks similar to one another. Even the president works within a smaller context much of the time with the staff and administrators who directly report to him or her. Within each small group, people socialize with one another, learn from, consult with, and gossip with one another. In this interaction, they learn to assign meaning to what is happening around them. So it is important that you not only understand the saga of your college in general, but also understand how people in smaller units behave and think.

There is fascinating research showing how individuals who think of themselves as part of a group can influence one another. For example, in a study conducted in the mid-twentieth century, Peter Blau found that the attitudes of social welfare workers toward their clients were affected by their colleagues. Welfare workers who worked in units with favorable attitudes toward their clients became more client-oriented; welfare workers assigned to "anti-client" units became more critical of their clients (Blau 1960, 178–193).

This is not an isolated example. Cass Sunstein, a professor of law at the University of Chicago, summarizes the results of diverse research on the influence of peers on the behavior of individuals in *Why Societies Need Dissent*. Some examples:

- Employees are far more likely to file suit if members of the same work-group have done so.

- Teenage girls who see other teenagers having children are more likely to become pregnant themselves.

- Broadcasters mimic one another, producing otherwise inexplicable fads in programming.

- The level of violent crime is greatly influenced by the perceived behavior of others in the community.

- Members of Congress pay close attention to the cues sent by their colleagues, often following the consensus position of those whom they trust, especially on issues outside of their own areas of expertise.

- Whether and how people plan for retirement is much affected by the behavior of others in their work group.

- The academic effort of group students in New England is affected by their peers, so much so that random assignments of first-year students to dormitories have significant consequences.

- In deciding whether to adopt new technologies, including high-yielding methods to produce rice, farmers are greatly influenced by the decisions of their peers.

- Lower courts follow one another, especially in highly technical areas, so judicial mistakes may be self-perpetuating. (Sunstein 2003, 10)

Sunstein's analysis of decisions of federal judges may be especially pertinent to colleges and universities. In their autonomy, federal judges are somewhat like tenured faculty members with job security. However, in other respects they have substantially more autonomy and, for this reason, one might think that they would be even less subject to the opinions of their peers. They undergo no significant peer review; their salaries are not determined by their colleagues. They are appointed for their competence as well as their political perspective; and they are typically in middle age, with well-established views, when they are appointed. Nonetheless, they are very much affected by their peers.

Sunstein studied three-judge panels, identified whether judges were appointed by a Republican or a Democratic president, and evaluated their voting behavior as liberal or conservative. As expected, the judges appointed by a Republican or Democratic president were, respectively, typically conservative or liberal. In settings in which two judges were from one party and the third from the other party, their behavior changed. The judge who was out-numbered two-to-one voted more like the members of the other party. Sunstein refers to this as "ideological dampening." Occasionally, the behavior of the outnumbered judges became so affected that they essentially joined and agreed with the members of the other party. Sunstein calls this the "reversal effect." When all three judges were appointed by a president of the same political party, their liberalism or conservatism was heightened. Sunstein refers to this as "amplification" (Sunstein 2003, 166–193).

These findings parallel the behavior of work units within universities. Within the university's overall saga, there exist the cultures of each work group. Because university departments are, to use Robert Birnbaum's phrase, "loosely coupled" (Birnbaum 1988, 38), the sub-culture of the department is especially influential on faculty members' behavior.

As with the example of the judges, people, even unconsciously, are influenced by their colleagues—influence that may be unrelated to their competency in their shared discipline. As with the judges, collective decision-making may take on the character of key individuals and the group can work together more harmoniously or in a more conflicted way even with relatively small changes in personnel. Although Sunstein's research led him to conclude that the tendency to conform within work groups stifles innovating and healthy dissent, I do not believe that this is inevitable. You can strengthen those aspects of the organizational saga that encourage dialogue, and reinforce this healthy behavior at the small group level when it occurs. You can be attuned to the influence of key individuals in their small groups, working with them—often individually—so that they can understand your vision, and in turn, affect their group.

KEY INDIVIDUALS

For eight years I lobbied in the Wisconsin State Capitol for the University of Wisconsin–Madison. Proposals were adopted or blocked in the majority caucus. Caucus members met in a large room. As with every group, most legislators sat in the same chair at the same table for each meeting, sitting with legislators with whom they got along socially and politically, and who tended to see the world as they did. At each of those tables of fifteen legislators, there were always two or three people who were very influential with others at the table. They were not necessarily formal leaders. I knew that if I could persuade those key individuals to support my amendment, I was likely to get a majority of votes. One table's key people might use policy arguments to persuade their colleagues. Another table's key people might rely more on personal relationships. Recognizing this, I also knew how best to craft my approach to them.

At the Capitol, there was an organizational culture with sagas about "how we do legislation in the Wisconsin Capitol." There were formal leaders at the front of the room (like the president of your faculty senate) who needed to be formally engaged. There were caucus tables (like your academic departments), each with its subculture and ways of getting things done, and each with its one or two key people who affected the others in the unit. Finally, there were leaders at each table — who were not necessarily the formal leaders, but who might be individuals with informal influence, winning the confidence of their colleagues in different ways.

Identifying Informal Leaders

These key individuals are likely to be "Connectors," as Malcolm Gladwell coined the term in *The Tipping Point*. Gladwell writes, "What makes someone a Connector? The first—and most obvious—criterion is that Connectors know lots of people. They are the kinds of people who know everyone. All of us know someone like this. But I don't think that we spent a lot of time thinking about the importance of these kinds of people" (Gladwell 2000a, 38).

Connectors are not necessarily people we think of as leaders. They are, rather, people that others listen to. They are well liked and respected. They make recommendations about books, restaurants, and friends and, in very informal ways, affect the behavior of people around them. They bring people together, often trying to reach resolution of conflicts. In higher education they are the individuals who know people in other academic departments. They tend to be on the "inside" of the institution. Their self-image, and the image others have of them, is that they care about preserving and advancing the university, not simply getting their own way.

The older Connectors are people who perpetuate the university's organizational saga, who tell the stories that define the institution. These Connectors probably have a perspective on all of the presidents who have been at the university for the last twenty or thirty years. People turn to them for a comparison of the new president with the leaders of the past. They are precious to the university, and they need to be supported and nurtured because of what they represent. They are important to you, for their support is crucial to the advancement of your ideas. The challenge is that they may be likely to want to keep things as they were, or at least as they remembered them. If you can get their support for change, you have made great progress.

One of your important early tasks is to identify these Connectors, to get to know them and their sphere of influence. In *The Tipping Point*, Gladwell describes the phenomenon he calls "tipping" and the important role that Connectors play in tipping. Tipping is a term that some readers may recall was used by sociologists in their study of neighborhood housing patterns in the 1950s. If a few black families moved into a white neighborhood, its racial composition did not change much. However, when a sufficient number of black families moved in, quite abruptly, almost all of the white families moved out. The neighborhood had "tipped." Gladwell studied tipping behavior in a wide variety of settings and subjects, from fashion to drug use and smoking. If certain people behave in a certain way, others are likely to follow. A surprisingly few people engaging in a new behavior can change the behavior of many.

What Gladwell calls tipping, Sunstein calls "social cascades." He writes:

> Cascades can involve judgments about either facts or values. They operate within legislatures, political parties, religious organizations, and the judicial system as well within countless groupings of citizens. When people are united by bonds of affection, the likelihood of cascades increases. Sometimes moral judgments are a product of cascade effects. (Sunstein 2003, 54)

Cascades can cause judges to follow the rules of other judges, doctors to prescribe the same medication because a few others have started doing so. Sunstein points out those cascades can be good or bad, and cites as example the freedom movement in South Africa that dramatically changed the government very quickly (Sunstein 2003, 55–56). You need Connectors, in short, to facilitate the "tipping" process. But you may embrace the sagas, know the subcultures, recognize and nurture the Connectors—and still be unable to bring about change.

THE TIME, ISSUE, AND CONDITIONS MUST BE RIGHT

Gladwell believes that a certain "context" must be present for such changes to take place. Two examples will illustrate this. Gladwell writes that the book, *Divine Secrets of the Ya-Ya Sisterhood*, did not sell especially well when it was released in 1996. Yet, by 1998 it was on the bestseller lists, where it stayed through 48 printings and 2.5 million copies. It began to sell, slowly at first, when an older generation of female readers gave it to their adult children who bought it for their children. Sales were unrelated to a major marketing effort—indeed, the marketing effort began *after* the book started to sell so well. The readers were influenced by their environment: the context of friends and relatives buying the book for them and urging them to buy it and read it.

The 2004 Presidential election activated thousands of conservative Christian churches to support George W. Bush for president, churches that also played a role in putting language outlawing gay marriage or civil unions on the ballots of eleven states. Most analysts credited Karl Rove, Bush's political advisor, for leading this effort. However, discussions with people throughout the country after the election revealed that, while Rove may have started the effort, most of the work was done in a decentralized way as people heard about other people's efforts. Indeed, the religious leaders were described as moving faster than Karl Rove. The context had been changed by the sanctioning of gay marriages in New York, Massachusetts, and San Francisco. The new context tipped the behavior of thousands of people around the country (Cooperman and Edsall 2004). The context had changed again by the time of the November 2006 elections. Unhappiness with the war and congressional scandals affected the fortunes of George W. Bush and the Republican Party. While the Democrats worked hard and effectively to recruit good candidates, they were helped enormously by the ground shifting under the Republican Party.

In these examples it was more than simply context and Connectors that caused the change, it was the right time. The *Ya-Ya Sisterhood* was very meaningful to women of several generations at a time when women were recognizing the importance of their interconnectedness. The year 2004 saw an intensely competitive national election at one of the most partisan periods in our nation's history. In the first instance there was an informal network of mothers and their daughters across generations. In the latter instance, there existed a more formal network of religious groups, somewhat independent of the Republican Party, that facilitated communication across denominations and across cities.

For change to occur conditions must be right. Sometimes these are conditions that you have helped create through your communication and leadership. Other times, external events create the conditions for change and as a leader you can take advantage of those conditions.

SUMMARY AND IMPLICATIONS

Understanding a university only through an organization chart, with its formal position descriptions and divisions of labor, is important, but not sufficient to successfully lead a complex organization. The culture of your institution has an enormous influence on the people who work there.

Organizations are places suffused with emotion, meaning, and values. It is through work and relations with colleagues that people obtain much of the meaning in their lives. These emotional aspects, while not explicitly rational or logical, can be very positive sources of influence in the work lives of individuals and in your direction for the university. The emotional attachment that staff have to their university can be called upon to provide individual sacrifices for the greater good of the organization. As should be obvious, employees are influenced not only by the people who are their superiors on the formal organizational chart, but also by others in their immediate work lives. Finally, only with the right context can you lead campus-wide change. Ideally it is a positive context, an atmosphere in which dialogue is valued, that you helped create through analysis and careful communication with both the formal leadership and with the Connectors.

With all of this in mind, it should not surprise you that research on leadership reveals that successful leaders see their universities as ambiguous; they see themselves in the *center* of their organizations, not on the top; and they are seen by their colleagues within the universities as influenceable. Imagining yourself in the middle of the organization, not simply on the top, is itself an idea of such fundamental ambiguity that you may think of it as an early test of your comfort with your job.

This chapter has emphasized that behavior in organizations is complex, and understanding and influencing it is difficult and subtle. However, human behavior is not random, and it is not irrational. Just because people are influenced by many factors and people does not mean that they reject leadership. In order to be successful, you must not only understand but must embrace these historical, extra-rational, non-hierarchical, informal aspects of university life. Understanding and embracing them will help you to establish the working environment, the context, that makes it possible for these bright, highly specialized colleagues to join in creating the best conditions for learning and teaching for its students.

Chapter 5

Understanding Leadership

Beyond the Job Description

None of us majored in presidency. We prepared, yes, but the degree is not granted until we retire.

Anonymous College president
(quoted in Penson, *Establishing the Presidency,*
Establishing the Base, the First 500 Days)

It is said that one military man remarked soon after his election as president of a university: "What kind of a place is this? I give an order and nothing happens. People pay no attention to what I say, or reply that they will take it under advisement. I ask for an opinion on how to proceed, and I get fifty different opinions. I propose what I think is a capital idea, and it produces a faculty wrangle. How does a man get things done in a place like this?

—Thomas Elsa Jones, President, Fisk University,
Earlham College (Jones et al., *Letters to College Presidents* 1964)

What Is Leadership?

Understanding your organization and its culture are essential but not sufficient if you are to become an effective leader at your university or college. This chapter seeks to help you move beyond understanding to successful leadership.

Visit any bookstore today. The sections on management or psychology are filled with books on how to lead. Ambitious business people read them on airplanes. One study found that the buyers do not read about 80% of these books in their entirety (Mickelthwait and Wooldridge 1996). These books often contain a good idea or two that could be described in a short article or monograph but they are oversold as solutions for larger issues.

Phil Rosenzweig, in his book, *The Halo Effect*, analyzes and describes serious flaws in even the most popular and best regarded books on leadership, including, *In Search of Excellence, Built to Last*, and *Good to Great*. The authors of these books identified and studied successful companies and identified what they believed to be common characteristics. They then described those characteristics as the reasons for their success.

Rosenzweig writes, "Each one claimed to boldly go where no research had gone before, to do what had never been done, and to have a greater claim to the truth. By the time we get to the last two, there are grandiose claims about virtual guarantees of success and immutable laws of physics" (Rosenzweig 2007, 127). And, "Not one of them recognized the central problem that robs them of validity—namely, that by relying on articles from the popular press, on business school case studies, and on retrospective interviews, their data were compromised by the Halo Effect" (2007, 128). A number of the companies exalted by these authors have experienced difficulties. The authors, however, are doing very well. Indeed, they command speaking fees of from $85,000 to $150,000 per speech!

There are the books that tell dramatic stories of leaders taking over troubled organizations and leading them out of difficulty to greatness. The leaders are invariably decisive and charismatic. The stories are exciting, if somewhat daunting. Rudy Giuliani, former Mayor of New York City, had been ridiculed in the press and his effectiveness as mayor had become quite diminished. Yet 9/11 inspired him to a great leadership for that specific event and for the days immediately following that attack. When Giuliani ran for President of the United States in 2007 and 2008, he focused almost solely on the events of 9/11 and his response to it. He came in third in the only primary in which he competed and dropped out of the race for the nomination. Winston Churchill inspired Great Britain's courageous fight against the Nazis. Still, he was voted out of office very shortly after World War II. These riveting examples of charismatic leadership take place at times of great crises. The stories are so compelling that people come to believe that charisma is a necessary trait at all times, and think that all of their problems can be solved if only they could just find the right leader who will inspire greatness. But leadership is rarely about charisma.

Another type of leadership book is highly prescriptive and breaks the job into small parts. These books are attractive because they suggest that while leadership is technical and complicated, it is understandable and can be mastered. Just the sort of thing that a new president, likely a former college professor, will find seductive! Total Quality Management (TQM) was such a system in the 1980s and 1990s. It is effective when applied to certain offices or programs where each part of an administrative process can be isolated, examined, and improved. However, systems like TQM work best in organizations where authority is centralized. As Robert Birnbaum has written, in higher education the authority is diffuse and the parts of the university are loosely coupled, so TQM is not effective and enthusiasm invariably fades away (Birnbaum 2000).

In fact, systems like TQM are less about leadership and more about management. Most presidents manage more than they lead. Because presidents were most likely managers in previous positions, it is tempting for them to resort to the familiar, especially when they are under pressure. The failure to understand the difference between leadership and management make it likely that you will be a modal president, as described in Chapter 1.

John Kotter, business professor emeritus at Harvard University, succinctly compares and contrasts management and leadership. Management is about doing things right. Leadership is about doing the right things. While both are essential in a successful organization, Kotter describes most organizations as over-managed and under-led. In *The Forces of Change* he compares management and leadership behavior in four areas (see Table 1).

Leading an organization is not about designing a management system like TQM. It is not a series of techniques that can be easily learned in a book, including this book. It takes insight, reflection, thinking, talking, trying new things, revising, and admitting mistakes. Describing these characteristics does not make exciting reading on an airplane. However, these traits are present in effective leaders.

The Authority for Leadership

Before I can discuss the instincts and skills I perceive in the best higher education leaders, I want to talk about where your authority comes from. There are two kinds of authority, formal and informal, sometimes described as "position power" and "personal power." These two categories are not entirely separable and you need to be conscious of both.

Formal leadership is bestowed upon you by the governing board. In a public institution, this board may be appointed to guide your individual institution or to govern the system of which you are a part. The board is typically appointed by the

	Management	Leadership
Creating an Agenda	Planning and budgeting: Establishing detailed steps and timetables for achieving needed results, and then allocating the resources necessary to make that happen	Establishing direction: Developing a vision of the future, often the distant future, and strategies for producing the changes needed to achieve that vision
Developing a Human Network for Achieving the Agenda	Organizing and staffing: Establishing some structure for accomplishing plan requirements, staffing that structure with individuals, delegating responsibility and authority for carrying out the plan, providing policies and procedures to help guide people, and creating methods or systems to monitor implementation	Aligning people: Communicating the direction by words and deeds to all those whose cooperation may be needed so as to influence the creation of teams and coalitions that understand the vision and strategies, and accept their validity
Execution	Controlling and problem solving: Monitoring results vs. plan in some detail, identifying deviations, and then planning and organizing to solve these problems	Motivating and inspiring: Energizing people to overcome major political, bureaucratic, and resource barriers to change by satisfying very basic, but often unfulfilled, human needs
Outcomes	Produces a degree of predictability and order, and has the potential of consistently producing key results expected by various stakeholders (e.g., for customers, always being on time; for stockholders, being on budget)	Produces change, often to a dramatic degree, and has the potential of producing extremely useful change (e.g., new products that customers want, new approaches to labor relations that help make a firm more competitive)

Table 1. Creating an agenda
(adapted from Kotter 1990)

governor. Private colleges and universities operate with a governing board typically chosen by other board members. Presidents tend to think of formal authority when they think about their jobs and they wish more such authority was available to them.

The willingness of a board to support the leadership of a president depends on their confidence in the competence of that individual and how regularly and candidly the president is keeping them informed of what is going on at the university. It also depends upon the kind of response the president receives, both internally and externally.

IMPORTANT UNDERSTANDINGS

As I think about college presidents whom I have known who were strong and effective leaders, I see a pattern of traits that they share. These, I believe, are the characteristics of leaders that are worth pondering. None is presented as a recipe. In Chapter 1, I said that an effective president knows himself or herself, and this self-knowledge is key. The next step is applying that knowledge to your job in a way that is comfortable for you. This idea is most easily understood by considering craftspeople.

Baseball is a craft. Players throw, bat, and field in a way they have learned over many years. All baseball players adhere to certain shared principles, and yet they apply those principles in a way that is affected by their training, body type, height, and other individual factors. Their athletic techniques may vary widely. Yet the best among them are graceful and their work appears effortless. Potters, too, learn difficult and exacting techniques, often over many years. All potters use similar materials and equipment. Two potters of equal quality create two vessels that are quite dissimilar. And in the work of the great potter a personal vision is evident. So it is with effective leadership. Two people may know the same management techniques, but their leadership styles may be different. You must both know the theory but apply it in a way that is natural to you. To do otherwise is exhausting, and you will appear so unnatural that people in the organization will sense it at once and their discovery will make you vulnerable. You are almost guaranteed to fail.

In his important book, *Intuition, Its Powers and Perils*, David G. Myers describes how quickly the mind can work of people with great aptitude in a field, with many years of training and experience. He said of master chess players, "Unlike a poor chess player who has few patterns stored in memory, a good player has 1,000 and a chess master has roughly 50,000. A chess master may also perceive the board in several chunks—clusters of positions that they have seen before" (Myers 2004, 54).

For my dissertation, I studied a university president over several years. The president had made a great many changes in a short period of time. I observed that many people thought that the changes were not that significant. One of my key advisors responded: "Think about Copernicus. When he said that the sun did not revolve around the earth, but that it was the other way around, nothing changed. The sun still came up in the morning. However, in another way, everything changed."

Finally, a strong leader knows the importance of reflecting, talking, and listening, and knows that these are sometimes more important than acting. A former baseball player told me that in trying so hard to be successful, he was forcing the game. "The coach taught us to let the game come to us. Let it unfold and we would know what to do." When presidents become frustrated and can't seem to get people to do what they want them to do—they often try to force things. Instead, they should be listening and diagnosing, letting the organization come to them before they act.

Ways of Thinking

Effective leaders are able to think about and understand five important things.

BEING INSIDE THE CULTURE. I have already discussed the importance of understanding the culture of your college: its history, its values, strengths, vulnerabilities, and heroic stories or organizational sagas. To lead an organization effectively you must become a part of that culture. You must understand it, embrace it, and work within it to lead it in its day-to-day accomplishments and establish goals for ambitious, long-term accomplishments. The people in the university need to think of their president as one of them. Of his role as Prime Minister during World War II, Winston Churchill said, "I was not the lion, but it fell to me to give the lion's roar."

Of course, the president is at the top of the organization in formal and important ways. However, in his study of presidents and the presidency, Edward Penson found that effective presidents do not view themselves at the top of the organization but at its center (Penson, *Establishing the Presidency, Establishing the Base, the First 500 Days* n.d., 5).

This approach recognizes the complexity and ambiguity of the organization and the diverse sources of influences on its members. It is not conceptually easy, and can cause you personal discomfort. It reduces the social distance between you and the members of your college community, for example. It places greater responsibility on you to communicate beyond the cabinet, including anyone in the college community. It requires political and analytical skills to assemble and make sense of large amounts of complex information that is often contradictory. Being in the center makes clear to you that opinions are diverse and that agreement on goals among constituents is often ambiguous.

BEING OUTSIDE OF THE CULTURE. At the same time, you must be separate from the organization. Because you are the primary person communicating with the external environment—alumni, parents, legislators, board members, donors —you must be able to represent the college in a way that they can hear and understand. And in turn, you must be able to communicate to your university community what you are hearing and learning from the larger environment in which the university exists. That is an important step in helping your organization respond to its environment. You are a translator.

The translator role is crucial to your success and, sometimes, to your survival. For example, the faculty at your university and your board of governors probably view the university and your responsibilities as president very differently from one another. You must keep both informed about the university in a way that is honest and accurate, yet also acknowledges the differences in how these crucial constituencies view the organization, their job, and yours.

Absorbing the culture of a university, and yet standing apart from it, is not easy but can afford important insights. Robert Park, an early twentieth century sociologist at the University of Chicago, wrote a classic article about what he called the "marginal man," someone who has one foot in one culture and the other foot in another. Being "marginal" can make it possible to have insights that someone entirely absorbed into a culture might not have (Park 1928). A few examples of "marginal men" illustrate the importance of living in two worlds and moving effectively between them.

In *Black Like, Me* by John Howard Griffin, the author, a white man, underwent chemical treatments to darken his skin. *Black Like Me* reports on his experience of being a black man in the South. Black men, of course, have written on this subject, but *Black Like Me* relates how it is to live in both worlds. This offers insights that a white man could never have achieved otherwise (Griffin 1989).

Another example comes from American history. We marvel at the wisdom and insight of our Founding Fathers who successfully led a revolution and created a constitution that has served this country for over 200 years. However, luck is not sufficient to explain the success of our democracy. Bernard Bailyn described the Founding Fathers as "provincials" in *To Begin the World Anew*:

> Never having been fully immersed in, never fully committed to or comfortable with, the cosmopolitan establishment, in the crucible of the Revolution they challenged its authority, and when faced with the

problems of public life they turned to their own local, provincial experiences for solutions. …They adhered to the facts of everyday life, and from them developed a fresh vision of what might be accomplished, what might be created. …

They attacked head-on the over refined, over elaborated, dogmatic metropolitan formulas in political thought, challenging assumptions that only idiots, they were indeed told, would question. (Bailyn 2003, 8–9)

In *Bobos in Paradise*, David Brooks reports that outsiders authored several of the most influential books of the last half of the twentieth century. Jane Jacobs was a young staff member for *Architectural Digest* when she wrote her seminal work, *American Cities*, in the early 1960s. Planners and urban politicians study Jacob's book today. Betty Friedan was what we used to call a homemaker with no advanced academic training in the social or behavior sciences. Still, her book, *The Feminine Mystique*, provided an alternative way of viewing the role of women in America, and helped provide the underpinnings of the women's movement in the United States. Rachel Carson was a young science researcher when she wrote her book, *Silent Spring*, about the degradation of the environment and the use of dangerous chemicals. Her name became synonymous with the environmental movement in the last forty years of the twentieth century (Brooks 2000).

In the mid-twentieth century, what was most effective and important about our American cities received little attention. The women's movement had not yet begun. There was little public consciousness about the effects of chemicals on our environment. Jane Jacobs, Betty Friedan, and Rachel Carson were young and obscure. Also, they were women working during a time when opportunities for women were extremely limited, when even accomplished women were typically not taken seriously. Their obscurity, their gender, their relative lack of formal training, and their youth made them marginal in their fields. They were not completely a part of the professional or organizational culture about which they were writing.

Earlier, I mentioned Alexis de Tocqueville. Two centuries after his visit to the young United States, we regularly cite the insights of this French outsider. Outsiders often see in ways others cannot. It is not easy to view the organization as an outsider, and it is particularly difficult if you have lived your professional career almost wholly inside the organization. However, to be effective as a leader, you must understand, and be able to empathize with, external views of higher education and your college in particular. Moving comfortably between the two worlds, living gracefully in each, and translating all the while, is an important skill. It is a lonely position, because it is easier to simply embrace the values and idiosyncrasies of your university. But doing so will make you less effective.

SEEING THE UNIVERSITY WHOLE. Entomologists informally classify the taxonomists in their discipline as "lumpers" and "splitters." Lumpers see similarities among the insects they are studying. Splitters look for differences. Successful presidents are lumpers, seeing similarities and wholeness, even if their previous academic success was due to their ability to split things into smaller pieces.

You must build bridges between these academic islands, finding common elements among people and ideas. When successful presidents establish goals for the organization, for example, they often do so by synthesizing aspects common to various departments or units that are ready for change. They identify newly developing areas of academic study which are growing in student demand, board and legislative support, and they link those emerging demands with existing and potential strengths within the university. They understand the university in broad, complete terms. Only then can they make sense of their responsibilities and communicate to the world how the college—not a single department or a single professor—matters.

BUILDING A COMMUNITY. The leader does not build a community. However, you help create conditions that make it easier for the many people in the university to build the community. We saw in Chapter 4 that people long for community, and that a strong community meets basic human needs. At the beginning of Chapter 2, I quoted a famous story about Daniel Webster's emotional presentation to the Supreme Court in the 1800s, in his defense of Dartmouth. Webster later acknowledged that he had been emotional and engaged in hyperbole. Nonetheless, it is a strong reminder of the role that sentiment for an organization can play. Indeed, sentiment towards an organization may be even stronger in the twenty-first century because it is not met elsewhere in our lives. Attachment to a tribe can trump other loyalties.

During crises people experience the things they hold in common. Consider the terrible days following 9/11. People who were stranded in Manhattan were taken in by strangers and provided comfort and housing. Thousands of citizens throughout the country gave so much blood that blood supply centers had to ask people to stop donating. People throughout the country wore Yankee baseball caps to show their support. The President of France, however improbably, even declared that the people of his country were Americans! New York City, at least for a while, became a community. The goal in leading an organization is to help people realize those commonalities even when a crisis is not present.

Our society is one of specialists and professionals. We have delegated to others what we used to do ourselves. MDs have replaced midwives. The professional army has replaced the draft. While these changes toward professionalism have brought technical improvements, they have done so at the cost to community, and in fact may actually increase the longing for voluntary association. The voluntary commitment to one another builds strong "social capital," in the words of Robert Putnam and Lewis Feldstein. In *Better Together* they write, "As used by social scientists, social capital refers to social networks, norms of reciprocity, mutual assistance, and trustworthiness" (Putnam and Feldstein 2003, 4). They continue, "Whereas during the first two-thirds of the twentieth century Americans were becoming more and more connected with one another and with community affairs, the last third of the century witnessed a startling and dismaying reversal of that trend. Beginning, roughly speaking, in the late 1960s, Americans in massive numbers began to join less, trust less, give less, vote less, and schmooze less" (Putnam and Feldstein 2003, 4).

The human need for identification with a group is so strong that it can be created artificially. Franz de Waal, an anthropologist, reports on an experiment in which participants were randomly assigned different colored badges, pens, and notepads labeled "Greens," and "Blues." "All they were asked to do was evaluate each other's presentations. They liked the presentations by people with their own color designation the best" (de Waal 2005, 134).

What does this mean for you, as president of a small college or university? Many faculty and staff members have chosen a smaller university because they were searching for a collegial experience. And freshmen are seeking a community that replaces the network of friends and family that they knew before they came to college. A university is an intentional community whose members join voluntarily. You cannot will a community into existence, but you can help create the conditions for a strong community to develop, helping to move people from the isolation of their department to thinking about issues across departments.

You do that by creating a context for trust and commitment and by choosing goals that reflect the real needs of the university, as well as its best hopes. Helping the collection of faculty, staff, and students at your university become a community is a significant source of influence for a university president.

FINDING MEANING. The importance of residential communities is obvious. What may be less obvious is the importance of work communities for relationships, support, and meaning. Earlier, discussing organizational sagas, I noted that Burton Clark declared that those organizational sagas, even weak sagas, "can compensate, in part, for the loss of meaning in much modern work" (1972, 179).

Clark wrote almost forty years ago. What was true then is even truer today. Since the 1960s, as I described earlier, opportunities for Americans to feel they are a part of something larger than themselves have continued to diminish. As community life for Americans has declined, work and the workplace have become more important. Charles Handy, in *The Age of Paradox*, notes, "The workplace has been the central community in the lives of many in this century" (Handy 1994, 260).

How, then, can you accommodate and nurture this natural hunger for meaning in the workplace?

First, effective presidents recognize the sagas associated with the university's history. You have an obligation to understand that history, and an opportunity to call upon that history to help the organization respond to new challenges. You need to make clear to your constituents that the organizational saga is what is guiding you as you make your decisions. Even when the history of a university is not as distinctive or compelling as that of Antioch, Reed, or Swarthmore, it can be powerful. Your challenge is to take your saga—which invariably points to your university's strengths—and translate it into a contemporary call to action, a call to rise to the challenges of today. The saga moves your college through time, creating continuity from its founding into the future.

Handy notes that it is the sense of continuity that makes possible a call for sacrifice today in order to achieve the goals of tomorrow (Handy 1994, 257). He also writes that "We need to re-emphasize the fact that institutions can be immortal even if we are not" (1994, 254). By calling upon the immortality of your institution, it confers a sort of immortality upon its members, too, when they participate in its story. Presidents honor their university by treating it as if it will go on forever and that you are its steward for a short time in the history of the organization. As president you will make better decisions as a result. You will lead by example, noting, calling on, and modeling the high standards of your organization's sagas.

Second, effective presidents recognize that financial rewards in small colleges and universities are often modest and that faculty often trade salary for satisfaction in their work. After arduous training, they seek affirmation of the value of what they have achieved, and of what they do. Faculty research, class preparation, and teaching are typically solitary, and lead to isolation. In small universities, a faculty member may have no colleagues in his or her specific discipline, no one to talk with in detail about the subject matter they are teaching. This does not diminish the need to feel that they are part of an organization that has a purpose; in fact, it may enhance it. They want their contribution to fit into the larger goals of the organization, something bigger than themselves. They expect the president to identify important goals, goals worth committing themselves to, and to describe those goals clearly and compellingly.

Third, effective presidents set high standards. Colleges and universities are filled with faculty and staff with high expectations for their work and the work of their colleagues. It is your job to behave in a way that greatly increases the likelihood that such conditions will prevail. You require it of the students, why not for everyone else at the university?

Finally, effective presidents build an atmosphere of trust. Trust creates the environment in which meaning can thrive. Today in the United States there is widespread concern about the decline in respect for authority and a decline in civility. Factions seem concerned about single issues rather than the common good. Trust of corporations, civic organizations, churches, and government has been declining for decades and is at a new low (Roberts 2004). Leading organizations under these conditions is difficult, and leading an organization whose very foundation must be based on trust, on accepting and, indeed, welcoming differences of opinion, is especially difficult. However, the very fact that these conditions exist has caused a great human longing for its opposite and people long for trusting relationships. The president who can create trust between people, among departments, between faculty and administration, will create the possibility for meaning within the university community.

These are the general understandings and ways of thinking about leadership. In the next chapter, I write about how to translate those understandings into goals for your university. Thinking and understanding before acting—not a bad mantra for your presidency.

Chapter 6

Success

How Do Some Presidents Achieve It?

I do not believe that any man can lead who does not act...under the impulse of a profound sympathy with those whom he leads —a sympathy which is insight—an insight which is of the heart rather than the intellect.

—Woodrow Wilson
(cited in Wills, *James Madison* 2002, xvii)

The essence of a President's persuasive task with congressmen and everybody else is to induce them to believe that what he wants of them is what their own appraisal of their responsibilities requires them to do in their interest, not his.

—Richard Neustadt
(*Presidential Power* 1962, 34)

Sailing a ship across the Pacific is no different from organizing a college or university for performance improvement. In both instances, it is immensely helpful if we can come to some agreement on which way to aim the pointy end.

—Daniel Seymour
(*Once Upon a Campus* 1995, xix)

Relating to the Organizational Saga

Effective leaders understand their organization and they view it in ways I described in Chapter 5. Such an understanding is derived from careful and continuous diagnosis of your organization. In this chapter, I want to describe some specific activities to help in such a diagnosis.

Build on Strengths

Every institution has strengths. For some, the strengths are historically strong academic programs; faculty, staff, graduates, and community members know what they are. For others, the strengths lie in a strong commitment to liberal arts programs, athletics, community service, or effective work with students needing special attention.

While your organization's history tells what the college has done, you should focus on what the college has done *well*. This connects to one of the deepest values in higher education: the excellence and meritocracy that the faculty and staff bring to their work, which resonate with the American public. To identify your college, as well as your own administration, with its historical excellence is a good place for a president to begin. Be sure to learn if there is a history of the university, even if unpublished.

As you read the institution's history, and as you listen to members of the college community and the public as they recall episodes and people, and hear stories about critical incidents in its history—echoed in often-used slogans, captured in school songs, displayed in the trophy cases—you can identify the parts of the organizational saga that capture your institution's story of excellence. Your challenge is to build on the meritocracy of the past in your contemporary goals for the institution, and to communicate these goals to the university community in a way that excites and motivates people, and persuades them that you understand them. This can be one of the most exciting and rewarding aspects of your job.

It is easy to get distracted by the negative aspects of the organizational story. We never have enough money, the system administration has not treated us fairly, and we are unappreciated by the local community. This latter is a typical mantra of faculty and staff (and not an appealing one: when things were going badly, Bill Clinton would sometimes complain about how hard he was working in order to do the right things for the American people, and how no one appreciated his efforts). It is easy to get caught up in these complaints, for people think that leaders should "fix" things, and you naturally want to demonstrate solidarity with your community and your skill at addressing issues. But you cannot succeed by spending all of your time on complaints. Some faculty and staff have come to those positions over many years and with much hard work, and your personal pep talk or inspirational speech will not change them. Movie producer Sam Goldwyn said about critics, "Don't pay any attention to them. Don't even ignore them."

Instead, shift the conversation back to the larger context, back to the qualities and the programs that exemplify excellence for the university, keeping in mind that the majority of people know that *they* will succeed if their university does better. Only by doing this can you bring along people who are not happy. And you do not need to bring them all along, nor should you expect to. You do not need unanimity to lead an organization, only a solid majority who are prepared to join you in moving the university forward. They will provide you with good advice and will talk positively to their colleagues.

Effective presidents are constantly alert for ideas, both from people inside and outside the university, which they can then weave into the organizational saga, showing how they relate in a contemporary way to the meritocracy of the past. They integrate these ideas and their own ideas, into compelling goals that are understandable and attractive. They make an appeal to the greater good, calling for individual contributions and sacrifices. If you deeply understand your institution, people will make the sacrifices when you ask them to join you in making changes.

Having crafted your goals in a way that resonates for your community, you can then behave in ways that impress on the university your understanding of the challenges in meeting these goals and your personal willingness to provide leadership in addressing them. When I was president we needed to increase student recruitment. I joined the academic vice president in personal visits to principals and guidance counselors at over fifty high schools throughout the state. While I have no illusion that this alone recruited significant numbers of students, we made it clear to the college community that this was such an important goal that we were willing to make a direct contribution, through a large commitment of time, at some hardship to ourselves. It made it easier to then exhort the admissions staff as well as the faculty to play their part.

Create a Positive Context

It takes the work of a great many people to accomplish most of the changes at a university. The effective president creates a context that makes it easier for everyone at the university to contribute and to feel part of the team. While increasing the number of students, developing a new major, or revising the core curriculum are tasks largely accomplished by the work of academic staff and faculty, your role is crucial. You must champion the importance of meeting a given goal and lend visible personal support, but—perhaps most important—also create a spirit of community and trust so that people will be motivated to help find solutions.

When I was president of a small college, we developed and approved five new degree programs after more than thirty-five years without new majors. A proposed computer science major had languished for nearly fifteen years after several unsuccessful efforts to reach consensus. A proposed interdisciplinary environmental studies degree required much difficult intellectual work and agreement on contentious issues about required courses. I made clear to the faculty that if we were to develop these majors, it was up to them to design the content, working with the academic vice president. Thus I let them know that they had the support of the president's office, and that I trusted them to do the right thing, and by doing so, the faculty conceived a program of which the college is proud.

Another important change during my presidency was a dramatic increase in fundraising. Of course it was essential that I hire the effective fundraiser that I did; but the role that I played was to communicate regularly with our alumni and community members about activities and progress at the college made by faculty and staff. My communications to them were reinforced by what they heard from people they knew on the faculty and staff. A clear majority in the college wanted to make progress and work together, and was happy to talk to their friends about it. President, fundraiser, faculty, and staff, sharing a vision, behaved as a team—which had not been true before—because the context had changed.

This attitude was of great benefit for our college. A major building was proposed, to be funded by the state. We expected that state approval would be at least a year in the future. I received an unexpected call from our lobbyist, who had just had a conversation with a key committee chair. The chair wanted to move the project up on the priority list, making it possible for us to receive funding a year earlier than we expected. The lobbyist reported that the committee chair, who was related to a staff member at the college, said "I hear that things are going well at Western these days." An informal comment from someone within the college was more credible than all of the written documents and testimony from me or the lobbyist.

In *The Contrarian's Guide to Leadership*, Steven Sample writes that "You as a leader can't really run your organization; rather, you can only lead individual followers, who then collectively give motion and substance to the organization of which you are the head" (Sample 2003). Sample described his role as President of the University of Southern California when the Rodney King riots exploded in the area surrounding his university. "I walked around and showed the flag, so to speak. I shook hands, chatted with students and staff, asked questions, listened to people tell their stories, and gave out copious compliments and reassurances. Everyone thought I was in charge, making seven decisions a minute, but I really wasn't. Instead, all the decisions were being made by people who had been trained for months in the handling of a catastrophic emergency" (Sample 2003).

A former university president described the job of president as one of walking around the campus, putting water on ideas that were not good and putting fuel oil on ideas that needed and deserved encouragement. This involves constant interaction with a great many people throughout the university, obtaining and providing information to people so that they can help to identify problems and solutions to problems. It is subtle, elusive, and ambiguous—but achievable.

RELATING TO PEOPLE

Delegate Most Decisions; Make the Important Ones

Most people think that presidents make many important decisions. The university's constituents support some of them. Others are opposed. Eventually, this thinking goes, the president's credibility is used up. Effectiveness is impaired. Finally, the president has made so many people unhappy that he or she must resign or retire and indeed there are those who believe that few presidents are able to remain effective for very long. While this is certainly true of United States presidents, whose influence fades significantly during their second term, this is a pessimistic view of leadership, and it need not be the case with you. In fact, influence waxes when you take action in an arena in which you already have a great deal of support, and wanes when you make a difficult decision in an arena where you may not have majority support. To be effective, you need to pace your decisions, spreading out the difficult ones, saving your influence for when you need it the most.

There is a more complicated, but much more dynamic and accurate way to view decisions. To best understand the subtlety and complexity of this process consider the presidents of the United States. They typically come into their jobs with a reasonable degree of credibility and a mandate to implement at least some of the policies on which they campaigned. If they generate significant public support, Congress is unlikely to resist passing legislation in support of the president.

When Franklin D. Roosevelt took office in 1933, the country was in a deep depression and the Hoover administration had refused to act. Roosevelt was able to pass a great deal of legislation early in the administration, typically by overwhelming majorities. When the U.S. Supreme Court ruled in 1935 that some of his legislation was unconstitutional, Roosevelt tried to get his own appointees on the Court more quickly than permitted by the constitution. Congress, the media, and the public viewed this as over-reaching, and he became a less powerful president. Then, after the Pearl Harbor attack in 1941, the American people looked to him for leadership and he responded strongly and immediately, and became a stronger president.

Occasionally, events over which you have no control will strengthen your authority. George W. Bush was a president elected without a majority and without a clear mandate, and so did not experience the usual honeymoon that U.S. presidents generally enjoy. But because of the 9/11 terrorist attacks, his authority was dramatically strengthened.

There are many relatively easy, popular decisions that build your influence. Successfully pursuing policies that have strong support makes your position stronger. So does choosing courses of action that are consistent with the long-established ways of doing things. Fundraising for a popular program, adding an academic major that has strong faculty and student support, or securing state funding for a new building, are unlikely to make any important constituents unhappy.

I like to think of the president operating within a circle. Most things the president does are not controversial and can be seen as occurring within the circle. Making decisions and leading within that circle is relatively easy. It is a conflict-free zone. The line that forms the circle is a membrane. When you make decisions or choose goals that require the university to do new and difficult things, things which may collide with the membrane and bump into important aspects of the organizational culture, you need to do so carefully, only selecting important changes, and communicating about those choices fully and in advance.

You may have only a few such opportunities during your tenure and whether successful or not, those are likely to define your presidency. If successful, they leave an important legacy of leadership. Wise leaders do not choose too many such goals, or they will accomplish none of them. However, a president that pursues *no* difficult goals will merely be a caretaker and will have lost significant opportunities to make the university better.

One of the most important aspects of decision-making is learning when and if to make them. If you delegate properly, providing real authority to your colleagues, they will make most of the decisions, as they should. The only way your colleagues can acquire the authority they need is because you provide it to them, and others on campus observe and experience their important decisions. A senior colleague may know more about a particular issue, and probably have a longer and deeper background in the subject than you do, in any case, so they *should* be the person to make decisions in that area. Steve Sample asserts that presidents should *avoid* making decisions if they can. This behavior sends a clear message that you truly value staff and are willing to delegate to them. When the president does get directly involved and makes a decision, it sends a message that a particular subject is important.

Faculty and staff want a leader, in spite of what you may see as evidence to the contrary. They want to participate in decisions and provide their ideas, but they also want a leader who will make the difficult decisions. If the loudest people on campus influence decisions, the rest of the campus community will become very uneasy about the process. Leaders do not make final decisions because of such pressure; they make them because they are convinced that they are utilizing the best information available.

Good leaders make what I call "information-based decisions," not "authority-based decisions." You should gather the people in the meeting room who have the necessary information, regardless of their position. You should seek the best information on a given issue, and make the best decision based on that information. Faculty, staff, and others want to be confident that you are making the best decisions for the university.

Being Influenceable

Steve Sample claims: "The average person suffers from three delusions: (1) that he is a good driver, (2) that he has a good sense of humor, and (3) that he is a good listener" (Sample 2003). Every president I have known thinks of himself or herself as a good listener. Talking with a president's colleagues often reveals a very different story.

Here is what they too often see. Presidents typically listen a lot when they begin their job. But soon they want the university to take new directions, especially their own new directions. Then, they begin to do more of the talking. In their enthusiasm about the ideas and their frustration that people do not seem to "get" their ideas, they begin talking a great deal. This trend continues throughout the presidency. And presidents learn, perhaps not consciously, that a way to avoid hearing things they do not want to hear—especially criticism and opinions different from their own—is to talk all the time so that people never get a chance to disagree with them.

There is a related problem of arrogance. You may begin your job as president fearing that you do not know enough. After you have talked with people, and spent some time on the job, you still feel that don't know enough, but that you know more than anyone else. Eventually, you may come to believe you know everything. Daniel Ellsberg, a former member of the National Security Council, described his early days at the NSC. Henry Kissinger told him that during the first six months on the job he would have access to information on subjects that he had been writing about for years. Having that information, he would learn that many things that he had written were wrong. Kissinger predicted to Ellsberg that he would feel stupid. However, after six months on the job, after having access to materials that others without security clearance did not have, he would know much more than his former colleagues. Then, Kissinger predicted, he would come to believe that *everybody else* was stupid. The dangers of incumbency are several and this is one of the most serious.

Birnbaum's long-term study of presidents revealed that the most successful presidents are what he describes as "influenceable." People will not only notice whether you seem attentive when they talk with you, but also whether anything ever *results* from the discussion. Effective presidents listen, they sort out the validity of what they hear, and then they act on what people tell them.

You must seek out individuals on your campus who you respect and who are respected by others as well. People who will tell you what they think. People who may view the world differently from you. Invite them to your office and ask them to talk to you about what is happening on campus. Vow not to talk for the first fifteen minutes, except to ask questions for clarification.

Political Skills

As president you work with groups of constituents who believe their interests and programs are of paramount importance. Academic departments or groupings of departments in the liberal arts or professional schools—all of whom have external connections to constituencies in business or music, art or theatre—lobby the leadership for more resources and recognition. So do alumni groups and athletics. Some are connected to accrediting bodies and other external bureaucracies, to graduates, occasionally to board members, as well as to students and student groups. Parents are not usually organized, but they may place pressure on the university for special treatment of their sons and daughters. The borders of the campus are blurred. If you see these as intrusions and wish they would go away so you could do your job, being president may not be the job for you.

These are best understood as political pressures that require political skills on your part. Presidents are often surprised at this important part of their job and some view these political demands as "dirty," unseemly, and beneath them. Many may yearn for the time when they can get those responsibilities "taken care of" and return to the important task of academic leadership. That time never returns, if it ever really existed, and the presidents who do not learn that fail. Bart Giamatti, former president of Yale University, noted:

> The job of a president is political, with competing demands for resources and attention. Especially in a time of limited resources and increased scrutiny of what colleges and universities do, presidents who do not bring political skills to the job, or who do not quickly acquire them, will not succeed. (1990)

It is most important that you understand that the university is not separate from society with a membrane protecting it from outside influence, but rather is a part of that society, responding to it, accommodating it and, importantly at times, resisting those outside pressures. A skillful president, who understands both the needs of the university as a whole and the art of politics, can be effective in keeping unwarranted political interference outside of the university.

There are several important ways to deal with political pressures. Part of your job as president is to elevate the discussion of issues so that they are understandable and important to everyone. If you do that effectively and honestly, putting individual issues in the context of the greater good and the long term interests of the university, you can count on the support of those seeking honest leadership, even though your position may not satisfy a given constituent group at a particular time.

An important part of these deliberations is to be careful to separate matters of principle from day-to-day decisions that involve short-term considerations. Presidents can make decisions of two types in this area, both problematical. Some presidents define virtually all decisions as matters of great principle—especially those that reflect their position. As Sample writes, you must decide which hill to die on (Sample 2003). If, on the other hand, you view everything as a matter of tactics and you simply satisfy the last powerful individual or constituents who talked with you, you will have a great many people talking to you all of the time.

Legislators whose positions typically waiver a lot receive the attention of a great many lobbyists who want to be the last person to talk with them before the vote. If you do that, you will lose your moral authority. On the other hand, principles are too important to be evoked all the time, every day. You must sort out what is truly that important and what is not. One way to act on this idea is to remind yourself that you do not usually need to make decisions immediately. You can often let people know you want to think about it or get more information. A good night's sleep, or even a restless night's sleep, can often avoid a decision you will regret. Do not allow yourself to be rushed.

Communicate

Presidents must communicate in two directions. They communicate *within* the campus community on a regular basis. And they communicate about the university to *external* audiences—donors, alumni, community members, board, and legislators. In both instances, they must carefully describe what is happening at the university and why, and how the people in the audience can be of help.

Effective leaders are the link between the outside environment and the university. They provide this link by careful explanation—not by the "Fidel Castro form of leadership" which is about blaming others. Just as Castro blames the United States for his country's problems, so do some presidents blame legislators, faculty, students, and board members. Blaming provides short-term relief, but in-termediate- and long-term unhappiness. It creates frustration and a sense of hopelessness on the part of your constituents.

One of the most common and serious mistakes you can make is to assume, often unconsciously, that your colleagues are concerned about the same things you are. This is rarely true. When faculty and staff go to work on Monday morning they are concerned about their very specific jobs, jobs that are often challenging and difficult. They do care about the university and how it is doing, but the big picture is typically not on their minds, as it is on yours. Their daily concerns become meaningful when they are linked to the goals of the larger organization. For that to happen, you must tell them about the goals and the larger picture. You must be an effective communicator, explaining both yourself and the issues the university is confronting. Because you cannot assume that you and the audience share values, experience, and knowledge, you must not "start in the middle" when you talk to them. You must start at the beginning and create a context for the issue you are going to discuss.

If you want them to respond to your leadership goals, you must talk about those goals in clear and convincing language. If there is a problem looming in funding, enrollment, or another important matter, begin laying the groundwork early by describing the situation, the challenges, and what you are doing to address the issue. People have an impressive ability to understand and accept difficult news, but they want the facts; they do not like to be surprised. Internal newsletters in which you address substantive subjects are important. In addition, regular talks and meetings with the faculty leadership, and occasional meetings of the campus community as a whole, are important. Be sparing about campus-wide meetings, for they connote crisis, and if the campus perceives the leader describing everything as a crisis, quite soon they will conclude that nothing is a crisis.

A common communications mistake of leaders is to confuse questioning about a proposal or decision as opposition. I have seen many presidents roll their eyes when they talk about "the faculty." The implication is that they have all sorts of good ideas to move the university forward, but the faculty is in opposition. The presidents imply both that they lack adequate authority and that faculty have narrow interests and oppose change. Sometimes, of course, this analysis is accurate, but at other times it may reflect discomfort with questioning or challenging. This is one of the quickest ways to isolate yourself, and eventually you will be talking only to those who agree with you, or who are reluctant to disagree, and bad decisions are the inevitable result.

Presidents often fail to recognize that the faculty are asking "why?" not saying "no." They are not thinking all day about the issues you are thinking about and they do not have all of the information you do. It is your job to explain the issues as early as possible so they have a framework for understanding your thinking. Here is the ideal way to present an issue (recognizing that the ideal situation is not always possible):

- An issue will soon face the university that will require action. Here is how it came about and here are the forces and people involved.

- The issue will require a response on the part of the university. Here are the choices I am thinking about. I will be consulting with you, formally and informally, on these alternatives and seeking your suggestions.

- By a certain date, after careful consultation, I will choose a course of action, announce it, and explain why I acted as I did.

75

Certain important decisions, such as personnel issues, cannot not be discussed publicly. Sometimes time is short and you must act now and explain later. However, if you provide a thorough explanation after the fact, when you can, it is very helpful. Even if you cannot, I have found faculty and staff to be accepting and understanding if you have consulted thoroughly and explained carefully on other issues. You will have built up trust and credits and most people will understand that your goal is protecting the university's best interests.

When you describe what you did and why, you must also describe what it *meant*. One of the reasons leaders lose their way and end up simply being managers is that they focus on small things all of the time. When they describe issues, they do so in the narrowest, most factual of terms. When you discuss issues, elevate them to a level where they fit in to the larger goals of the university and can make sense to people, even those who are not deeply involved in that particular subject. Your role is to provide the meaningful context for their work that people seek.

Address Conflict

The inability to recognize and address conflict is a road to failure. If you are to be a successful president, you must acknowledge conflict and, even if you are not comfortable with it, you must address it. Conflict falls into two categories. There is the conflict that occurs between other individuals that you must be prepared to mediate. You need to learn to identify those conflicts that are more than healthy, strong disagreements, going on too long and making it difficult for those involved to work together. The conflicts negatively affect the university. Mediation skills are important.

The other type of conflict involves you directly. Some are unavoidable. For example, you may have inherited budget problems or need to cut programs and you will receive many conflicting views about what to do. You need to define the issue clearly, consult broadly, act, and then explain what you did and why. Do not blame others for the situation you are in. It will get some short term sympathy, but making difficult decisions is part of being president.

Other conflicts that involve you are ones in which you take steps to improve or maintain the university. These are at least occasionally inevitable if you are to move the organization. They may be difficult personnel decisions, such as terminating a staff member or denying tenure. They may involve making a decision that you are convinced is right, even though you do not have majority support.

With these decisions, make sure you have consulted with the right people, have explained yourself, and are not simply being stubborn. Avoiding difficult decisions, as a way of avoiding conflict, is likely to generate greater conflict and make you even more uncomfortable and the problem greater. Keeping unqualified staff, for instance, sends a message to the university that you accept mediocrity, even while you are talking about excellence. You lose your moral authority to uphold the high standards you expect your colleagues to adhere to.

Whenever I had to make a difficult decision, I pictured myself explaining it in a public situation, to the board, the media, or to a meeting of faculty and staff. If I was convinced it was the right decision, even if it was one with which not everyone would agree, I experienced a degree of comfort. If I was not sure it was the right one, I was uncomfortable. This is one example of many in which doing the right thing and living with yourself coincide and make the best policy.

A Key Survival Skill

I am regularly amazed at search committee members who are certain that they understand job candidates after an hour interview. The reality is that although people may yearn for the ability to see people, ideas, or decisions as black-and-white, most are frustratingly subtle shades of gray.

You will receive a lot of simple and unambiguous advice from people, especially those not very familiar with the issues you are dealing with. (Lest we be too harsh on these advice-givers, we can reflect for a moment on the advice we ourselves give, perhaps daily, to U.S. presidents and football coaches, advice which is often emphatic and certain.) People seem to like to feel that they can cut straight to the heart of a matter. Your response to simple advice may be to tell the advice giver, or privately think, "if only you knew all of the players, the conflicting advice, the information, the subtleties." You may define the advice-givers as simple, in part, at least, to relieve anxiety that comes from ambiguity and act accordingly. This will get you into deep trouble.

A tolerance for ambiguity is a key presidential survival skill. Robert Rubin was with Goldman Sachs for twenty-six years and eventually was co-senior partner. He then served for eight years in the Clinton White House, part of that time as secretary of the Treasury. He has been a star in the private sector and in the highest levels of the federal government. After his service in government he wrote,

Some people I've encountered in life seem more certain about everything than I am about anything. That kind of certainty is just a personality trait I lack. It's an attitude that seems to me to misunderstand the very nature of reality—its complexity and ambiguity—and thereby to provide a rather poor basis for working through decisions in a way that is likely to lead to the best results. (Rubin and Weisberg 2004, xii)

Few decisions are black-and-white. With most important decisions you need to remain open to new information, get as many thoughtful alternative views as you can, try out your ideas on trusted individuals before you act, and then act in good faith, even though there may never be enough data to let you know, with certainty, what the right course of action will be. In explaining the decision, it is often wise to acknowledge that others in the university may disagree and that the decision was not an easy one.

CHAPTER 7

GETTING STARTED RIGHT

The First Year & Beyond

> Shortly after Terry Sanford, former Governor of North Carolina, assumed the presidency of Duke University, students held a demonstration on campus. One of the students implored the other students to march to the administration building and take it over. President Sanford took the podium and said, "Great. If you are going to occupy Allen Building, take me with you because I've been trying to occupy it for a month."
>
> —Terry Sanford
> (quoted in Barber, *Duke University Register* 1978, 2)

As president, you will be assuming what will almost certainly be the most difficult, challenging, frustrating, and rewarding position in your career. When you were a vice president or a dean, you had a job. Now, it often seems, you *are* the job. The chances of success increase greatly if you handle your entry into the university, and the first year, well. Of course, succeeding in the first year is no guarantee of long-term success. But a wobbly first year, when people are assessing who you are and your competence, is not simply a bad way to start. You may experience problems from which you will not recover.

Whatever your academic training or professional background, you will be undertaking responsibilities that you have never had before. You will be performing these responsibilities in a more public setting than ever before. Invariably, you will experience some surprises. So will the people affected by those decisions. When you become president, you make decisions that affect many people, often in important ways. Your decisions will affect people you know only vaguely, or not at all. People will assess you with very little information. They will not only focus on specific decisions you make, but also on you as a person: your competence, your dedication, and your ethics and values. Is this fair? Maybe not, but these are the same sort of assessments that you and I have made of others who have affected our lives.

We all behave in ways that are obvious to those around us, and not so obvious to ourselves. To be a successful president you must learn to see yourself, including how you view the world and how others see you. We all have an imperfect understanding in these areas, of course, but the better the understanding, the more likely you are to be successful. As you make decisions, you will better make sense of your own motivation and the reactions of others. What follows are amplifications of these ideas.

What People Notice

ASSUMPTIONS ABOUT PEOPLE. The assumptions you make about people with whom you work have a great effect on how your new colleagues will react and the tone that you set early in your presidency. Some presidents assume that their colleagues are competent unless they demonstrate otherwise. Others wait for their colleagues to first demonstrate their competence. The implications of this distinction for presidents, and the people around them, are enormous.

Each of us takes different approaches to the trustworthiness of people and their motivations. The bases for these assumptions are deeply rooted, and are derived from our view of the world and how it works. The goal here is not to change your assumptions (they are unlikely to change anyway), but to understand that you have them, and to encourage you to examine yours, so that in knowing this about yourself, you can better understand why people respond to you the way they do.

HOW YOU COMMUNICATE DECISIONS. A second trait to be conscious of concerns your decision making. Each of us thinks about and approaches decisions differently. Some of us are reflective, asking questions and finally coming to a decision. Others try out ideas early, speculating about possible answers and approaches. Still others come to quick conclusions, speaking casually on important subjects. While close colleagues recognize how you think and may accordingly treat your early thoughts as speculative, people who only occasionally meet with you will invariably take seriously off-hand comments and speculative remarks. New presidents are often stunned and irritated that the way they have worked for their entire careers is now causing problems. Lawrence Summers, president of Harvard University, was casual in his remarks about women and speculating about their aptitude in the sciences, assuming he was in a private conference and that those in attendance would understand he was speaking tentatively. The president of the most prestigious university in the world, tenured at an earlier age than any faculty member in the history at Harvard, and presumably aware of its culture, received more attention from that remark than any of his formal public comments. While this was not the only reason for his early departure as president, it was an important one.

Your colleagues at your university must adapt to the way you work and most of them expect to. However, you must go part of the way to meet them. You should understand how your approaches to thinking and work affect other people and the way they view you. What you do, and especially what you do early in your tenure, will have a long-term, likely permanent, effect on how you are evaluated on and off campus.

Because these assessments are often made with little information, the clues you provide to the organization and the community become very important. Communication must be carefully planned and clear because people tend to take very seriously offhand remarks, casually given interviews, and hastily written letters. We all believe (often with good reason) that informal, unscripted behavior is more "real," more "genuine," than formal presentations. People want to know what the "real" president is like; they look for evidence, however tenuous or flimsy. This suggests a need for maturity, insight, judgment, and an ability for reflection and listening. While we all like to think we possess these qualities—and surely we all do in some measure—these attributes are tested when you are the president. Even when you fail, on occasion, as you no doubt will, learn carefully from that experience.

THE STANDARDS YOU SET. Your standards about communication, candor, honesty, and excellence must be high. Only by establishing those standards for yourself are you are in a position to hold others to them. On the other hand, remember that early promises you make about communication will be remembered, and you will be judged accordingly. Jimmy Carter said, "I will never lie to you." He was one of the most honest presidents in memory. However, every time he held back information and did not, or could not, answer a question with complete candor, people remembered his promise. Further, as an engineer, he valued facts and detail. People knew this about him, so if he made a misstatement, he was held to that higher standard. Ronald Reagan had a very different approach. He spoke in large terms and metaphors. He regularly made factual mistakes in his press conferences and his staff issued corrections the next day. However, when the media derided him for the mistakes, the American people made it clear, by his impressive poll numbers, that they were judging him by a different standard. In both cases, the people knew the president's standards and judged him accordingly. To a significant degree, you will be judged by the standards you establish. Establish them carefully.

Early Promises. Do not make off-hand or premature promises. They will not be forgotten. George H. W. Bush said, "Read my lips. No new taxes." When the 1992 elections came, he was defeated. Forgotten was his masterful leadership in the Gulf War, or the fact that the small tax increase was credited by many economists as helping the economy. College presidents have made early promises to raise unrealistic amounts of private money, to build new buildings, and to attract more students. Even if you attract more private contributions, build more buildings, or attract more students than any of your predecessors, if you do not meet your publicly stated goals, you will be judged by the standard you announced for yourself. The standards you set should be inspiring but do-able, addressing real issues, new challenges, and old, neglected problems. Your goal should be to deliver *beyond* the promises you make.

Who Sees You, and Where. People in the university community will scrutinize your background. If you have a background in science, they will wonder if you know and care about the humanities. Which events will you attend as you get to know about student projects and productions? You will receive a high level of scrutiny. Be careful about the number of cultural, social, and athletic events you attend. If you are extraordinarily visible the first year, they will expect it of you the rest of your presidency.

Visibility can take other forms, too. I know a president who announced that she would spend a great deal of time learning and becoming involved in the details of each of the operations in the university, and having acquired that understanding, would then delegate more broadly. I know of another president who declared that because there was so much to learn about the university internally, he would not engage in external matters for a year. In both cases, waiting was unwise. People had drawn conclusions about both of them before the end of their first year—and those conclusions were accurate. One was a micro-manager; the other was someone who was much more comfortable staying on campus, in his office. They did not change that behavior after the first year.

What You Learn First. You have probably progressed through your career with a good understanding of one of the most important elements of university governance, where the most important work of teaching and research take place. This is, of course, the academic department. In subsequent assignments, you may have had the opportunity to learn about the larger academic world and the task of linking decisions to financial and other considerations. You have acquired an understanding of the complex, ambiguous, and decentralized nature of the college or university, and the subtleties required in leading such an organization imbued with the values of the university. But you may not have been involved with external relations such as fundraising, alumni relations, and communication with the news media; also, it is likely that you have had limited exposure to board relations. You may have had little experience in campus-wide budgeting, intercollegiate athletics, or student government.

While it is natural and more comfortable to spend time doing the things we know best, it is in the areas where your experience and familiarity are limited that you must concentrate initially, spending what might seem to you to be an inordinate amount of time learning about them. Seek out and listen carefully to the staff responsible for these areas. Your colleagues will notice that you want to learn, and to be comprehensive and fair to the entire university. Failure to learn the whole can easily cause you to founder later.

Be Yourself

Everyone associated with the university will wonder how you work and what you expect of them. They will figure it out over time. However, I have a better approach. Tell them, and then be consistent with what you said. Make clear how you approach your work, the degree of your accessibility, your commitment to candor and honesty, and your willingness to admit mistakes.

You can stretch yourself, you can demand of yourself more than you have in previous jobs, but ultimately you must be yourself. If you try to be someone else, someone you have never been, you will be discovered. There are dozens of football coaches in the country who tried to be Vince Lombardi and failed. They might have become second or third rate Lombardis, but they would have been better off—and would likely have made a much greater contribution—if they had been themselves. The same is true of the presidency. As Yogi Berra said to a young baseball player who was emulating the batting stance of a star player on the team, "If you can't copy him, don't imitate him."

People often confuse charisma with leadership. Yet the history of the business world is filled with examples of charismatic CEOs who came to the organization with big ideas, acted on those ideas without enough information or advice, and left the business behind in shambles as they went to another high paying position. As I noted in Chapter 5 leadership is rarely about charisma and most organizations do not need a charismatic leader most of the time.

The most obvious reason for not being concerned about being charismatic is that it will probably require trying to be someone you are not. That does not work. In addition, the focus in such an approach is typically on the leader, not the organization. A fundamental tenant of this book is that successful presidents focus on what the organization needs, not on the leader. Charismatic leaders are likely to want to make big changes to establish their leadership and to leave a legacy. Your university may not need big changes. The leadership it requires must involve a perceptive analysis of the organization and a focus on what it needs.

Charisma is typically associated with narcissism, impulsivity, and other characteristics not associated with solid, long term benefits for the organization (Vazire and Funder 2006). Robert Kaiser reports, "Four scholarly studies have examined charisma. Not a single one finds charisma and performance linked. The only thing charisma correlates to is a high salary" (Kaiser 2007). John Kotter, Harvard emeritus business professor, a respected writer on organizational behavior and leadership, writes that leadership "has nothing to do with having 'charisma' or other exotic personality traits" (Kotter 1999, 51).

Narcissistic people often make important decisions, especially personnel decisions, based on how those decisions will affect them and their presidency, rather than the needs of the organization. They resist suggestions from others because they believe that any advice they receive is not as good as their own judgment. They avoid acknowledging mistakes and inflate their role in successes. Because they make decisions with such confidence, others are likely to accept those decisions and they become excessively influential in groups. In his detailed study of presidents, Birnbaum concluded,

> There were only a few examples ... where charisma helped rather than hindered the institution, and it is likely that in higher education in general, charismatic leaders have created more problems than solutions. (Birnbaum 1992, 33)

Do not confuse charisma with the competence that your university needs. You must be well prepared, especially in your speeches, your statements to the media, and your written communication. Your colleagues need competence, listening, clear communication, clear expectations, integrity, honesty, willingness to make tough decisions, and hard work. These characteristics, taken together, have a charisma all their own. Over time, as things go well, people may attribute your good decisions to charisma, when those decisions are really the result of hard work, consultation, and good judgment. In a very short time, people in the university and community will have a sense of who you are. They will have talked about it with one another, sought information and confirmation. These conclusions, while tentative, will become increasingly firm. You can greatly increase the likelihood of success as president if you convey who you are thoughtfully, with clarity and consistency, in both word and deed.

LEARN ABOUT THE UNIVERSITY

Earlier in this book I talked about the imperative to know your university's culture. You need to have as much information from as many sources as possible. This means you must rely on far more than your senior staff—and they must understand that you will meet with people throughout the university, including people who report to them, and that this will not threaten their authority. You should get out of the office to meet with people where they do their work. This reduces the social distance between you and colleagues, and you are very likely to get better information. Also, it shows people you really do want to find out about them and what they do.

Listen carefully to all of them. As you get to know them, you will learn who can provide the best information, focused on the organization and not on their idiosyncratic agenda. This will provide perspectives that you need. As president, every time I visited people on campus, outside my office, often without appointment, I learned something. Most often, I returned to my office impressed with the insights of my colleagues, recognized that my efforts were appreciated, and—perhaps most important—I saw teaching and learning going on, unrelated to my worries about the budget or the next board meeting, which put my own issues in context. I always returned to my office refreshed.

As you wander around campus and meet people, most of these individuals will have formal reporting relationships to someone else in the university. You should assume that those deans and vice presidents who they report to will have some sensitivity about your establishing relationships among individuals for whom they believe themselves to be responsible. Those deans and vice presidents need to get over that, but they can do so only with your help. You need to be careful not to make decisions that bypass them. One of your most important responsibilities is to provide support for the other leaders on the campus.

Each time I assumed a new job I made available a simple questionnaire to faculty and staff. Although it could be completed anonymously if people prefer, it is helpful to know if the respondent is a faculty or staff member, and where they work in the university. In the questionnaire I ask what the university does well, what it could do better, and what they believe their new leader should do. I also leave space for any comments they would like to make, and make it clear that I welcome ideas from everyone. Invariably, I learned from these questionnaires and established in a concrete way my interest in getting information and advice.

Look for creative ways to find out what is happening at your new university. When Richard Rush was president of Mankato State University, he lived in a dormitory with the students for a week each year. When Donna Shalala was chancellor at the University of Wisconsin–Madison, she rode with the Madison police department one evening to see what kinds of problems they were experiencing with students. I would periodically join students for lunch in the dining hall. Occasionally, the meetings were awkward and the students shy. Other times they were animated and enthusiastic. (When a student with whom I was having lunch asked what I did, I told her I was the president. She said, "Of what?") I learned about how the university was doing in ways that would have been hard to know without such contacts.

Early in your presidency it is important to learn very quickly who is respected and who is known for being insightful and caring about the university. Bring those people together for lunch and ask them to tell you about the place they love. Spend time taking notes and asking questions. Although you should not yet be telling them what you plan on doing, it is a very good time to try out ideas and hypotheses that may be translated into initiatives on campus. Learn about the symbols and the history of the organization. The word will spread that the new president asked them to talk, wanted to learn from them, and did not interrupt.

In all of these efforts you are acquiring valuable information about your university, about who can provide sound advice, about who has a broad view, and who holds idiosyncratic views that do not represent the thinking of others. You are also making it clear that you care about the university to which so many of them have dedicated their careers. You are reducing the social distance between you and your new colleagues. In a small organization people should know you as a person, not just as "the president." When problems occur, as they will—or when you make mistakes, as you also surely will—they may be unhappy, but they will be unhappy with a person they know, not simply a symbol. If you permit yourself to become defined only as a symbol—the president—you will have squandered important opportunities to lead your university.

You will acquire a great many facts. Facts are not simply isolated bits of data. Your job as leader is to make sense of the facts and ask yourself what they mean. Having acquired that meaning you will be in a position to take steps to strengthen existing programs, fix problems, and take initiatives. While people will tell you a wide variety of things about the place they work and attend college, their insights and all of the facts are not random—they have patterns and meaning. One of the most fascinating, intricate, and exciting parts of your job is to understand that meaning and translate it into effective leadership.

DEALING WITH THE UNEXPECTED

As you settle into the job and learn more about your university, its history and culture, and current challenges, you will begin to identify courses of action you should take to lead the institution. If you are focused, as you should be, the major efforts will be about three or four important goals.

While you are busy identifying and advancing important and what may seem to be career-defining goals, something will almost surely go wrong. It may be a big, unexpected and messy problem. It may be a problem you inherited. It may be something that you had nothing to do with that simply happened on your watch. It may be a contested tenure decision or a misappropriation of funds. Controversy over the university's mascot. A critical audit. A controversial speaker. If yours is a public university, it may well be a reduction of funds for the next fiscal year or, even worse, during the current year. What can make it even more difficult to handle is that it may be in an area in which you are least familiar—not only involving an unfamiliar subject matter, but staff and faculty with whom you are not well acquainted.

Presidents almost invariably see these events as huge distractions that they wish would go away so they could focus on the "real" issues, the ones on which they have set out to make their mark. Commonly, they act slowly on this "intrusive" problem. They make a huge mistake. You must address these problems fully, carefully, and, after you are prepared, forcefully.

Everything you have conveyed to the university community about yourself before the problem occurred, both formally and informally, has been important to the community members. However, a big public challenge is the real test. People will compare what you have described as your approach to your work with how you actually behave. If you handle it the way you have described yourself, your stature and, therefore, your authority, will be enhanced and you will be able to accomplish other important goals—the goals you first set out to accomplish, that are more likely to be of your choosing.

As Chancellor at the University of Wisconsin–Madison, Donna Shalala wanted to improve undergraduate education and, in doing so, strengthen the bonds between the people of Wisconsin and the university. Because the football team was losing most of its games, it was also losing fans, and the revenue to the athletic department had declined substantially. Visible public programs that aren't going well cause people to wonder what else might be wrong at the university. After consultation with the athletic board, she fired the football coach and the athletic director. Because she made a wise decision about such a visible program in which so many of the citizens of the state were interested, she increased her visibility and credibility. This allowed her to return to focusing on undergraduate education with greater effectiveness.

When you handle such issues, you must understand that, while they may be unwelcome, you must address them, and they may represent an opportunity. You can demonstrate that you are in charge and will handle the problem; that you will consult with others; you will not violate either the large symbols of the institution such as academic freedom, or the local, idiosyncratic aspects of the university's history that are important. Do not forget, in spite of the limited authority of the university president, people want a leader.

As a new president, you have inherited a lot of good will. People want you to succeed. However, you will not have developed much political capital to call upon, so how you handle your first crisis becomes especially important. You are defining yourself.

COMMUNICATE CLEARLY AND CAREFULLY

Winston Churchill spent about an hour of preparation on each minute of the speeches that he delivered to the English people. Words are important in politics and they are important in academic leadership.

In your previous position, you shared a common vocabulary and references with the people you spoke to. As president, however, assume that you need to start from the beginning on the issues you are addressing. Do not speak in shorthand. Communicate regularly and with great care. Start at the beginning of the issue, not the middle. Send messages to the campus that describe your underlying assumptions and the context within which you are approaching important decisions. Define the issues clearly and, if possible, let people know with whom you are consulting and when you will make a decision. Do not overstate a problem, turning it into a crisis when it is not; this can only make the problem worse, and cost you credibility when a real crisis emerges. People will be paying attention to your messages, as they never have done before in your career. If you miscommunicate, you undermine the messages you want to send, and you have to spend valuable time trying to correct the confusion you have created.

Do not write or talk like a government or business bureaucrat, with jargon and acronyms; communicate in a way that people will want to listen to what you have to say—not simply because you are communicating about something important, but because you are clear, concise, and compelling. The people in the university want to be proud to have you as their spokesperson. You may not have very good writing skills. Find someone you can trust who does have those skills and ask them to be relentless in their editing of your drafts. Ask a trusted colleague to provide a brief critique after you make important public remarks. It is worth the time and personal discomfort. Communication involves not only conveying messages, but also receiving them. We all think we are good listeners. Most of us are not, especially when we become defensive and feel we are misunderstood. When you ask a question, especially if you are under pressure, make sure the person you are asking is done talking before you start to talk.

Leadership in a small university is a conversation that never ends. A conversation takes place between and among people who have real relationships. In healthy relationships, people affect the behavior of one another.

As important as how you communicate is what you communicate about. Talk with the university community and its supporters about important matters that they care about. Remember that they care about facts and make sure you have them straight. Remember, also, that the life of an organization is about more than facts. It is an important part of the lives of many people, so make sure that you understand and convey the emotional meaning about the issues. Make it clear that you care about the people affected by the issues and your decisions, and that you are taking those concerns into account. If, as part of that communication, you make a mistake or get the facts wrong, correct them publicly and quickly, taking responsibility for the error.

Choose Goals that Address the University's Aspirations

You will undoubtedly inherit issues that need immediate attention. However, take time to work on your own initiatives early, even if they are small. As I discussed in Chapter 6, think of yourself in the middle of a circle within which there is relatively little conflict. Within this circle, you can make decisions without much opposition and gather support relatively easily. Such activities can provide credibility and momentum.

When Nancy Zimpher became Chancellor of the University of Wisconsin– Milwaukee she collected matters of small but constant irritation to people on campus. The restroom in a particular building needed painting, a door handle was broken, the registrar's office was not open during the lunch hour. She fixed those little problems and strengthened her presidency.

At the college where I was president we had a problem with dogs on campus. Students would bring their dogs to school with them. They would tie the dogs outside the classroom or let them roam the campus. The dogs' barking irritated everyone and caused disruption on campus. During my fall speech to the faculty and staff I announced that we were going to do something about the dogs on campus. If a dog was spotted, the security office would be called, and a notice was put on the dog's collar that next time it would be removed from campus. Everyone, me included, was part of the dog patrol! Because people assumed that this was a problem they simply "had to live with," they were elated. I was amazed when I received a hearty applause when I made my announcement. We fixed the dog problem! On to other issues!

Three important lessons come from these examples. First, when you fix little things you develop momentum and credibility to address larger issues. Second, we all spend much of our time dealing with little things. When they are irritants and are fixed, we are grateful. Third, if you make a promise you had better deliver. I may have turned in more dogs than anyone else on campus.

The edges of the circle are where the more difficult changes are located. As president, you can take on only so many of these issues during your career and at any one time. Choose them with particular care, for they are likely to define your presidency. Only when you understand your institution well—its culture, values, and history—should you announce goals of this magnitude. They should be organic to the institution. You should privately try out versions of these ideas with people you trust, who are in different walks of life at the university. You should shape and reshape them until you get it right. Both literally and metaphorically, you want people to nod affirmatively when you talk about those goals because they know they embody the important aspirations not of the president, but of the university.

SOME FINAL ADVICE

DON'T CRITICIZE YOUR PREDECESSOR. As soon as you arrive on the job people will say things to you about the president who preceded you. Sometimes they will be letting you know what you should do differently. Sometimes they are criticizing your predecessor as a way of complimenting you, by contrast. Be careful. Do not denigrate the person who preceded you. While complimentary contrasts may be encouraging and make you feel good, people will see you as petty if you take them very seriously. In addition, no matter how unpopular the previous president may have been, that individual had supporters who will not appreciate your remarks.

SEEK HELP FROM OTHER PEOPLE EVERY DAY. Ask fundamental questions about why the university does what it does, and ask a number of people the same question. Do not confine this effort to your senior staff, but find senior faculty members, or emeritus faculty members to talk to. Call your colleagues at your previous institution, get to know other presidents who think like you and are at similar universities. Try out ideas on them.

DO NOT BRING YOUR OLD JOB WITH YOU. It is often difficult for academic vice presidents to leave behind the work that they love and that is so familiar. Often without being aware of what they are doing, they take much of their old responsibilities with them by looking over the shoulder of the academic vice president, perhaps even taking on some of that person's responsibilities. This is especially true if they are at the university where they themselves were academic vice president. Simply working harder and doing two jobs does not work. You will not do either job very well and you will drive your academic vice president crazy.

DO BRING YOUR OLD VALUES WITH YOU. You may still feel like the faculty member that you probably were, earlier in your career. You are the same person, after all. Still, the faculty will not see you as a fellow faculty member; they will see you as an administrator. It is still possible to retain the important values of the faculty in your administrative job. Over time, your behavior will reflect these values, and people will come to understand what you share with them. In the meantime, try not to take it personally when they do not.

WHEN YOU ARE STUCK, SLOW DOWN. Think about the problem over the weekend. Occasionally, when I would get stuck, I would ask myself to think like a consultant, coming to the campus for the first time with the clarity of the outsider. Then, on Monday morning, I would meet with a few colleagues and try out some new ideas. Not all of my ideas were good and they told me to forget them or they told me how to make them better. Sometimes my half-developed ideas inspired better ideas from them.

Try not to get defensive about the problems of your university as you are grappling with solutions. While you must often take responsibility for something that goes wrong on campus, even if you were not involved, you should approach the problems in the spirit of analysis, not defensiveness. Good solutions will rarely come when you are defensive.

NEVER GIVE YOUR AUTHORITY AWAY. I am not talking about delegating authority, which you *should* do. I am talking about abandoning presidential responsibility to make final decisions. You give away your authority when you accept and act on advice from a committee that you do not really believe in. You may decide to accept a committee recommendation when the issue is gray, as it fairly often is, or the stakes are small. However, when you are asked to defend a decision before the board, the campus community, or the public, you cannot say you did it because a committee, by majority vote, recommended it. It must be your decision and you must defend it. In fact, I used this explanation to committees occasionally in discussing a recommendation with them. This is a delicate and sometimes subtle business, because the committee might reasonably ask why you sought their advice if you then chose to ignore it. A discussion with the committee as they begin their work, and sometimes during their work, can help reduce the possibility of this happening, but cannot eliminate it.

One test you can apply is to ask yourself whether you are compromising an important principle. Never do that. It is even more important to be on the right side of an issue than it is the winning side (although that can only happen occasionally!). There are at least two reasons for staying with principles. The first is that people are watching what you do. They will appreciate your taking a difficult, principled stand. Another reason is that you need to live with yourself and be comfortable that you made a sound decision. You have committed to your university your time and much of your life—but you have not signed a contract to sacrifice your principles.

Another way to give away your authority surfaces during disagreements on campus. If you become entangled with an outspoken faculty member, for example, your strongest position is to always be, and act like, the president. If your disagreement becomes personal, if it appears that you are resorting to demonstrating that you are in charge rather than acting on a set of well-articulated principles, you have reduced the issue to two people in conflict, and your credibility will be reduced.

You Aren't Responsible for Solving Everything. Much of your job is to make it possible for others to lead, in areas where you can not and should not. In the fall, when I would make opening remarks to the faculty and staff about the new year, I would talk about new programs that I thought were important. One year I suggested to them that it would be presumptuous for me to tell them *what* to think. However, I wanted to suggest to them some things that I thought they should think *about*. Degrees in computer science and environmental studies had been discussed for years. I made it clear that I thought they were important programs and that I would support efforts by the faculty to develop the programs. When they were finally developed and approved, I gave the faculty credit—appropriately enough, because they did the work. The encouragement and commitment of resources was my role. Do not worry about getting credit yourself. People will know of your contribution.

Faculty and Staff May Not Want To Be Led, but They Want a Leader. That purposefully contradictory statement conveys what I believe to be the ambiguity and ambivalence about exercising authority within a university. Strong, clear leadership is reassuring to people in the university. People do not feel reassured if they suspect that the opinion of whoever talks to you loudest and last is the one whose advice you will follow. They want you to consult widely; they want clear explanations of your reasoning; but they want the decisions to be yours.

Erik Erikson, the psychoanalyst, observed, "The question is not whether you have a neurosis. It is whether the neurosis has you." Adapting that insightful remark, I would say that the question is whether you have a job or the job has you. Of course, sometimes the job will have you. Sometimes, someone else, or many others, will seem to be setting the agenda for you and your university. There will be days like that, or weeks. Slow down; delegate; remember that you are not the only one responsible for addressing problems; the vast majority of the people inside and outside the university want you and the institution to succeed. Involve more people in solving the problem; they will appreciate your asking. Spend a weekend remembering what it was that you were trying to accomplish before you got distracted. Start over again on Monday. Always keep trying out new ideas and then, before you act, listen to what people you trust have to say about those ideas.

CHOOSING & LEADING
YOUR TEAM

You Need Help

Motivation and inspiration energize people, not by pushing
them in the right direction as control mechanisms do but by satisfying basic human needs for achievement, a sense of belonging,
recognition, self-esteem, a feeling of control over one's life, and
the ability to live up to one's ideas. Such feelings touch us deeply
and elicit a powerful response.

—John P. Kotter
(*What Leaders Really Do* 1990, 60)

Efforts that don't have a powerful enough guiding coalition can
make apparent progress for a while. But, sooner or later, the opposition gathers itself together and stops the change.

—John P. Kotter
(*What Leaders Really Do* 1990, 80)

This book is intended to help presidents lead a university. It is important to remember, however, that you do not really provide most of the leadership of your
institution. You do not know how to do most of the tasks that need doing in the
university (although some presidents are loathe to admit it). These jobs should be
performed by those who can do them better. You must be free to do the job of
president. Steve Sample asserts that the president's most important task is to support the senior team as they accomplish the necessary tasks to lead and run the

university. The university may have an excellent strategic plan, but only with effective people to implement the plan can it move forward.

> Leaders don't really *run* organizations (although we often use that term in describing leadership). Rather, leaders lead individual followers, who collectively give motion and substance to the organization of which the leader is the head. The contrarian leader never loses sight of this fact, which is often a major reason for his success. (Sample 2002, 157)

Earlier, I discussed organizational culture and how important it is in shaping the values and behavior of people in the workplace. Organizational culture defines a way of doing things which often takes on an importance greater than what might be expected or justified. The behavior of the people who are on the leadership team—the senior leaders, the vice presidents, and a few others—set the tone for what happens each day at the university. They do it within the context of the atmosphere of trust and confidence you need to establish within the organization.

When your team members speak, people assume that they are speaking for you; or at least, that you agree with what they are saying, whether you are comfortable with this assumption or not. And, collectively, your team members know more than others about what is happening in the organization. You must rely on them to understand and make sense of that information. When you have a question that needs addressing, you start with your team members.

The people who report to you *do not work for you. They work for the university, just like you.* They report to you and you should hold them accountable for doing a good job but they are not "your people." Together, you are working to advance the organization. If you hire people whose identity and allegiance is primarily to you, they will not be the conduit to the university that you need to succeed. They must have standing and authority that they have earned through their competence. You have provided them that opportunity to demonstrate that competence; you have not hired them to serve simply as an extension of you and your office.

This critical idea may be made clearer by thinking about what occurs when a new governor or U.S. president chooses cabinet members. Invariably the team members are chosen because of their strong ties with the new governor or president. Governors and presidents may be engaged in a virtual hostile takeover of government from the career civil servants. The civil servants brace themselves for yet another administration, welcoming the new leadership if it sees the world as they do, resisting if it differs. You do not want to take that approach.

Too often, new university presidents are determined to "take over" their institution. They hire people whose loyalty is first to them, who know that they are there by the grace of the president. These presidents assemble a team of outsiders, with no institutional history, loyalties, or relationships within the university. The president and the team try to impose their image on the university. Not surprisingly, these presidents and their teams fail. As they struggle, they meet each week in cabinet meetings and agree that it is not their fault that things are not going well; the university is simply opposed to new ideas and change. Presidents who want to fill their cabinet with "their people" will soon be in the lonely position of working with a handful of people personally loyal to them, but unable to lead the university. So it is crucial to bear in mind that you are not choosing people for your administration; you are choosing them for your university.

What kinds of people do you need on your senior team? First, of course, they must have a mastery of the technical aspects of their job, whether it is curriculum, finance, student services, or fundraising. Their integrity must be impeccable and they must have the interpersonal skills to relate effectively to the people who report to them, to work with their colleagues, and to relate to you. They should work effectively in the organization, whether it is up, down, or across the hierarchy. I have a fairly simple tool that works well for me for evaluating effectiveness in establishing and maintaining work relationships. I call it the *100% theory of human relationships*. For a relationship to exist, both people must come together in a way that totals 100%. However, both parties do not necessarily make the same contribution to the relationship. You need people who are willing to go 70% or 80% of the way, recognizing that someone they must work with may be making a valuable contribution, but will only go 20% or 30% of the way in the relationship.

Of course, you will learn that your senior staff can't do all of these tasks equally well. In that, like you, they must know what they are not good at, and together you must make sure they have people around *them* who are good at those things.

BUILDING THE TEAM

You are working to establish an open, collegial atmosphere at the university, with an organization open to new ideas, and you must begin with your own team. You should seek a balance between a reasonable agreement about approaches and goals in your new administration, a compatibility that is essential, while avoiding "group think," where people are so similar and so compatible that they resist outsiders and new ideas. If you do not, then when times are difficult you will be spending time with people who view the world in the same way as you do, to the exclusion of other people and alternative approaches. This is a difficult balance to achieve. It should also be considered an ideal that may, in fact, not be achieved completely.

What should be the other characteristics of the people who are on your senior team? Ideally, there will be some people who have served in previous administrations, so they know the organization. Those individuals should be judged by the same criteria you use when you hire someone directly. They should be competent, effective, and loyal. If they are not—and it is helpful if you make that determination fairly early—you should not keep them. It is much easier to evaluate someone who is already at the university than it is to evaluate someone you are thinking of bringing from outside, because there is so much more information available—you can see them in action as well as assess their performance from others who know them. When you do receive such assessments, be careful to place more credence on the observations of people who really care about and represent the organization. Over the years, resentments develop and people can personalize their differences with colleagues. If a vice president made difficult decisions, but made them fairly, after full consideration of the consequences, this should count as an asset even if certain individuals felt slighted by those decisions.

You need people who tell you what they think. To make sure you get such advice, the most important person is you. You set the tone, making it clear that you welcome it. I always tell the management team that they have an obligation to let me know what they think, and I have a responsibility to make it easy for them to tell me and to hear them out. I also say that I do not want to find out after the fact that they had a concern they failed to express before I decided on a course of action. All of us believe that we are good at receiving advice, including ideas contrary to our way of thinking. In fact, most of us are not, especially when we have been on the job for a while, or are under pressure.

It is also important that the senior management team work well together. When you meet with them they should talk with one another, as well as to you. They should freely comment on and express opinions about one another's areas of responsibility. Again, you set the tone by inviting advice from them about subjects that are clearly within your responsibility and that they would expect you to make, such as board relations. If you want them to talk with one another, you must lead by example.

We are all more comfortable with people who are like us, but surrounding yourself with people like you does the university no good. I have seen organizations whose senior teams feel great about one another, offer warm mutual support—and consistently make mediocre decisions. It is important that you not mistake compatibility for effectiveness. Research on investment clubs, in which all members contribute a certain amount of money on a regular basis and then decide collectively how to invest it, demonstrates that clubs whose members are *not* personally close have better investment records than those clubs with closer interpersonal relations (Sunstein 2003, 2). The people in investment clubs are not unique. People hesitate to put their emotional investments with others—their friendships—at risk, and, often, however unconsciously, trade off candor for acceptance. In a work group it is a costly trade-off. Whether there are close personal relationships among team members or not, you must set the tone by inviting tough critiques of your ideas and engaging in those critiques yourself in meetings with your team. While they should work well together, they need not always agree. And it certainly does not mean that they must be close friends.

What other characteristics should you seek in team members? In addition to competence, good work habits, integrity, and willingness to give and accept critiques, you need breadth. If you expect team members to help one another, each needs to be effective within his or her job description, but also to know the university broadly. Thus the vice president for student affairs thoroughly knows student issues, but should also understand the concerns of the finance vice president. The finance vice president thoroughly knows finance, but should also be able to talk about student issues, admission standards, discipline policies, and other important matters. The academic vice president needs to be conscious of the many areas within student services. Most of the important issues require ideas and input from the team, not from a single individual. You cannot competently discuss scholarships without involving the student affairs officer, the development director, and the finance vice president.

If you expect people to work together effectively throughout the university, you and your team must show the way. When I came to my job as president I told the faculty and staff at the beginning of my first semester that I knew there had been problems with the cabinet working together effectively. I told them the changes would start with me and my senior team. We were going to model effective teamwork. If you hold other people to high standards, you must hold yourself to the same standard.

What should you do if a member of your team simply cannot do the job that you need him or her to do? If you must let a person go, treat that individual with dignity. You always want the focus to be on the *decision* and whether it was wise or not. You never want the release of that person to be seen as an arbitrary exercise of your authority, especially if people see personal feelings are involved. Remember, it is not about you, it is about the organization. You want to treat the person with dignity because it is the humane thing to do, and to do otherwise would reflect badly on your use of authority. There is another important reason. Your goal should always be to make the positions for which you are responsible, attractive. If you remove an individual in a manner that seems harsh and arbitrary, it will be more difficult to recruit a competent replacement.

I know a president who fired a powerful, controversial dean shortly after he began his presidency. Immediately, everyone began focusing on the president and his decision, not on the substantive issues surrounding the dean's performance. The president might have tried to work with that dean, obtained more information, or strengthened his position on campus before making such a controversial decision. He could have even told that dean he would be let go, but that he could remain in his current position until the end of the academic year. That would have provided time for him to find another position, and might have avoided a difficult and messy firing that fueled controversy around the president. That president lasted three turbulent years.

I have told people in October that they would not be renewed the following July, and that I needed to announce by February that we were hiring a new person. This provides time for the individual to begin a search for another position, and allows him or her to choose the timing of the resignation letter. If the person you are letting go wants a reasonable job reference, you should be clear that you expect hard work during the time remaining. If the person behaves badly, acting disloyal or publicly critical, you need to remove them sooner than the date you planned, but this rarely happens.

People are watching. One of the most elementary aspects of organizational life is that people talk about the boss. You and I did it as we worked our way up in the university. Why should we think that anyone else is different? Because the college is what all faculty, staff, and students have in common, decisions made about the college, and about the people who make the decisions, are common topics at basketball games, in departmental meetings, and over lunch.

As president, you are in your own way a teacher. You are teaching people about yourself, the expectations they should have of you, and the expectations that you have of them. Faculty and staff are very interested in what you say, especially when you arrive on the job. Ultimately, they are much more interested in what you do than in what you say, and they are always comparing them. The two had better be consistent if you want to succeed. Your colleagues will accept mistakes. (I know that from experience because I made my share.) But they will not accept hypocrisy, nor should they.

Evaluating Your Team

The typical method of evaluating staff is the annual review. Both parties talk about last year's performance and about goals for the coming year. Both take a deep breath, especially when there are concerns about performance and ability to do the job, and both are glad when the meeting is over. The supervisor turns in the report to the human resources department and both parties try not to think about the subject again until next year. While I am sure it works better than this in some cases, I do not find annual reviews helpful for the supervisor or the supervisee, or for helping to accomplish the university's goals.

As you might guess, I have an alternative. I believe that every day, or almost every day, is evaluation day. You should be letting the person who reports to you know, on a regular basis, how they are doing. You should compliment their work, and make clear where they need to improve. Also, you should ask the individual whether you are clearly communicating what you need from them. Think back to when you reported to a president, or someone else in authority. You needed to adjust to their way of doing business; but your supervisor also needed to adjust to yours. While the president's responsibility for adapting may be less, the president still must meet their needs. This is not coddling. It is respectful and humane and it greatly increases the likelihood that you will get the best work out of the person involved.

Leading and working with staff members involves establishing and maintaining a healthy relationship. In every relationship in your life—whether a friendship, a family member, or a colleague—your goal should be to bring out the best behavior of the people you are leading. You do that by acknowledging that each is different from another and responding differently, and appropriately, to each. Regardless of their differences, however, all people have important characteristics in common. We all require clear communication and expectations. We want to work with someone we can admire, who pursues goals of excellence with high integrity, who appeals to our hopes, not our fears.

Thus, the evaluation process depends upon the quality of your daily interactions and upon the standards that you hold yourself to. Still, there are "teaching moments," where you can spontaneously give feedback to the people who report to you. These moments are available after your colleagues, or you and your colleague, deal with an especially difficult issue. It can be a helpful time to discuss what principles were involved in how it was handled. People are looking for cues about your response to their work, especially early in the working relationship. Make your cues as explicit as possible. Getting your feedback into the open reduces their guesswork and anxiety and improves their work. It also makes the work more satisfying to them and the entire team will benefit, for there are few things as satisfying in life as working with an enthusiastic, competent colleague on a project. Such satisfactions can offset many of the often-difficult parts of the job.

Harry Truman, reflecting on his presidency, the difficulty of the job, and the self-interest of people with whom he worked, said "If you want friends in Washington, get a dog." Getting a dog may well be a good idea. They are, after all loyal. Indeed, they have been described as the Uncle Tom of the animal world. However, they are a terrible source of advice and know nothing about budgets.

Good team members are a wonderful source, not only of advice, but support. When people ask me how I like retirement and if I miss my job, I invariably tell them that I do not miss the work nearly as much as I miss my colleagues. A competent, loyal team (whose members have a sense of humor, I should add), can get you through some difficult times. They are also a great source of enjoyment and one of the major reasons for wanting to go to the office on Monday mornings.

CHAPTER 9

Working with Faculty

Why Don't They Get with the Program?

Every day of every year, year in and year out, the president must prove himself to the faculty. Especially in a large institution, there is no such thing as a completely cordial and trusting relationship. The president is, in some sense, the symbolic adversary, since he is ultimately the bearer of whatever bad news comes to the faculty these days.

—Theodore M. Hesburgh
(*The Hesburgh Papers* 1979, 11)

University professors never think of themselves as employees; they think of themselves as the heart of the place, as the texture of the place, as the essence of the place. And they are right.

—A. Bartlett Giamatti
(*A Free and Ordered Space* 1989, 43)

A free hand is the first and abiding requisite of scholarly and scientific work.

—Thorsten Veblen
(*The Higher Learning in America* 1918, 63)

I hope I have made clear throughout this book that effective leadership requires relating to and involving large numbers of faculty and staff at your university. It is true that without the presence of staff, the university could not function and this good work must be recognized. It is also true that teaching and research are the heart of your university and, while there are important differences among universities, faculty have a very special role in each. This is as it should be.

Working effectively with faculty can make the difference between success and failure in your presidency. To advance many of the goals of the university you need their strong support. Within the university, of course, this is obvious. But even outside the university, when you engage with legislators, your governing board, the alumni, you carry the university with you. Metaphorically, the faculty are in the room when you do that important external work. Further, those faculty may have talked with legislators, community members, and alumni who then are predisposed to judge you accordingly. As a practical matter, few presidents with the strong support of the faculty have been fired by boards.

WHY IS THERE TENSION WITH THE FACULTY?

Typically there is tension between faculty and administration. An extreme example of this is described by a former academic vice president.

> During my early days as a chief academic officer, I said to a faculty member as we passed each other on campus, "Well, hi there; haven't seen you in quite a while." Now, when I took psychology 101, that comment was a called a favorable "stroke" in that I took more than casual note of his existence. He apparently did not take psych 101.
>
> Within two hours I had a two-page, single-spaced letter on my desk, alleging that I had suggested that he was missing in action. He not only assured me that he was on Campus almost every day but then proceeded to recite his accomplishments, kind of a summary of his resume. The coup de grâce was the last sentence. "May I have a copy (sic) of your resume to see how much you have done." (Greenberg 2002, 1)

The administrative counterpart to this example is a public statement made by the president of a large public university to a public gathering of other university presidents. She said: "My goal is to get people to do what I want them to do and to have them believe it was their idea." These examples highlight the tensions that often exist between faculty and administrators, something I find especially ironic because so many presidents began their university careers as faculty members themselves.

I emphasized that when you arrive on campus, you need to spend time on things you don't know about—the budget, the physical plant, planning, athletics and external relations. This is appropriate. But because you may have been part of a faculty, and you know about a faculty's values and rhythms, you may believe that you can postpone your interactions with this university's faculty while you learn about the issues surrounding the new stadium. You do not want to be stunned, as so many presidents are, to learn that you may not have the support of the faculty, and that many faculty members do not see you as one of their own.

What typically happens next is that presidents and faculty both retreat into behavior that is initially defensive and ultimately is distancing and patronizing. Presidents respond to the lack of campus support by devoting more time with their governing board and other external constituents (Birnbaum 1992, 93). The worst stereotypical expectations of both the faculty and the administration are realized. The president concludes that the faculty can't be trusted. The president confirms that the faculty are out of touch with the larger world, don't really care about the well-being of the university, and the only way of accomplishing anything is to work around them. Meanwhile the faculty is affirmed in their suspicion that this new president, like the previous president, is out of touch with the day-to-day life of the university, is arrogant, enjoys power for its own sake, and doesn't really care about the well-being of the university.

Let's be clear that this is a challenge. Birnbaum's research makes clear that faculty support tends decline over the term of a presidency (Birnbaum 1992, 73). Many faculty members never acquire a broad, conceptual understanding of their institution, even when they are exposed to it. They lack interest, experience, and, sometimes, aptitude to see more broadly than their classroom or department. Indeed, the traditional university is organized to accommodate people who focus on their jobs, not the larger organization. The loosely-coupled structure of a university often creates a great social and psychological distance between a faculty member and the president. Finally, and literally, president and faculty understand reality differently. Myers writes, "We intuitively assume that as we see and remember the world, so it is. We assume that others see it as we do (false consensus). And if they obviously don't, we assume that the bias is at their end" (Myers 2002, 98; Keltner and Robinson 1996).

THREE KINDS OF FACULTY MEMBERS

With regard to their university orientation beyond their faculty work, faculty can be roughly grouped into three categories. There are those deeply involved in their work. They are very good at what they do, and they don't want to be distracted.

While they recognize they are affected by faculty governance decisions, they do not participate beyond voting for their department chair. They tend to see the university from the perspective of their department. They should not need to get involved in other matters beyond those of basic citizenship.

The next group has a somewhat broader view of their university, is active in department matters, and speaks out on matters beyond the department. The members of this group are often willing to serve on the faculty senate and other campus-wide university committees. They can be important glue in binding together parts of the university, as they can understand and appreciate other parts of the organization.

The third group—and you may have been a member of this group—is the smallest. They are the faculty members who have a natural aptitude for administration and leadership. They are chosen often and early for important committee assignments and often move into administrative positions.

Only a few faculty members aspire to administrative positions. Consider the term most often associated with becoming a chair: we say that the person is "willing." The position is rotated every several years because it provides an opportunity for department chairs to return to teaching before they get out of touch with their field. It is also rotated because many faculty members would not accept the assignment if it was for an indefinite period of time. Still another reason is that faculty members would be uneasy at having a colleague who assumed more authority for an indefinite period of time. This turnover can be advantageous for the university, as it increases the number of faculty who have had an opportunity to acquire a broader understanding of the university.

For most faculty members, serving as chair of their department is the most administrative experience they will ever have, and are likely to see the position as one in which their primary responsibility is to be an advocate for their department while not necessarily acquiring a broader understanding of the university. Because it is an introduction to administration, for those who like it and have an aptitude for it, this is an important route to other administrative responsibilities. These individuals need to be nurtured and encouraged to assume other leadership responsibilities within the university. But this group of ambitious administrators may also include frustrated faculty members whose careers are disappointments, wanting to advance in administration as a way of leaving behind their academic field and their colleagues. They will pose a special challenge for you for they may blame their unhappiness on the failure of the university (Burns 1955, 467–486).

Whatever category a given faculty member may fall into, in a loosely coupled organization such as a university, where authority is dispersed, there are two general things you must recognize, understand, and even sympathize with. First, the perspectives and daily experiences of faculty are very different from yours. Second, the faculty values their autonomy. The very fact that the academic department is loosely coupled to the rest of the university means that they and their academic department are able to function relatively autonomously. Understanding this, is it possible to effectively lead your university and have a collegial, and non-adversarial relationship with the faculty? I believe the answer is "yes," if you approach it deliberately and with care.

Two Key Things to Recognize

Although it may not always seem to be true, there are two certainties that can both guide your vision and sustain you when times are tough:

THE FACULTY WANT AN EFFECTIVE PRESIDENT. Some presidents have convinced themselves that most faculty think they don't need them. While it may seem that most of the faculty behave in a way that suggests they believe they would do fine without you, and that your responsibilities should consist of raising money for academic programs, recruiting good students (certainly better than are currently at your university, where the quality seems to be declining each year!), do not believe your worst fears. Those fears are both self-defeating and wrong.

THE FACULTY WANT TO BE PART OF A DYNAMIC UNIVERSITY. When faculty members go to work on Monday morning they are preoccupied with their lectures for that day, lab preparations, and papers that need grading. They may not think much about how or what their university is doing. However, they want their work to be part of something larger. As much as they might act as though they are in private practice, they want to be part of an organization that is going somewhere. Only you, the president, can provide that leadership.

What I Learned about Governance

I offer a few things that I have learned concerning all-important campus governance.

DEMONSTRATE THE IMPORTANCE OF PARTICIPATION IN GOVERNANCE. As I mentioned earlier, Birnbaum's research indicates that successful presidents are viewed an "influenceable," obviously taking seriously the reports of committees or of the faculty senate. Make sure that they see your commitment to strong, appropriate, collective campus governance. Do you notice well-regarded teachers and scholars participating in the governance process? If so, it is one indicator that governance is working on your campus.

Respect the Often Slow Governance Process. Provide ample time for committees to do their work. It will sometimes be frustrating for you, as it was for me. At the same time, you can introduce to them the world in which *you* work by letting them know what the board and the legislators are doing and how the timeliness of responses is crucial. With this understanding, they are much more apt to work quickly.

Improve the Quality of Governance. Governance provides guidelines for good decision-making and that is its justification. Governance should not convey "rights" on the faculty or any other group on campus. The reason faculty and others should participate in governance is because, with their help, the university can make better decisions. When faculty claim specific "rights" to make decisions, governance has devolved into a struggle between president and faculty for decision-making power. Changing, or at least moderating, this ethos may be one of your most important and difficult assignments.

There are undoubtedly times you have shaken your head about a recommendation made by a committee, perhaps one on which you served. You sometimes cannot defend the decision itself without describing the group dynamics that were involved, including the political trade-offs within the committee. As president you cannot accept such decisions on important matters and, equally importantly, you cannot, and—as I said earlier—should not defend them to the campus, your board, and the general public. As president I told committees to not tell me how *many people support a recommendation*, but why it was a *good idea*. Don't talk to me about the politics, convince me on the merits. To go further, I would try to help them understand the world outside the college. I could not tell my board that this decision had strong support of a committee on campus and that was why I was bringing it to them. The board does not care, nor should it. They want to know why the president supports it because that is who they will hold accountable. Committee recommendations are just that, recommendations. Ultimately, as president you must decide and you must be comfortable with making a public defense of the decision. It may come as a recommendation, but you must make it your decision. Simply because committee recommendations were on occasion not helpful is not a reason to rely on them less. Committee discussion is a form of democracy and, like all democracies, imperfect. However, democracies, through good communication, provide opportunities for improvement. When you reject a governance recommendation be sure to provide a good explanation.

Governance sometimes becomes a separation of powers, with the president representing the executive branch and the faculty the legislative branch. A few faculty like it that way. They can vote on a recommendation and not worry about implementation or the ultimate decision. Effective faculty governance, including promotion and tenure decisions, in which faculty are deeply involved, requires tough decisions that affect careers. If your behavior makes it clear to the faculty that you are prepared to make difficult decisions, the faculty are more likely to do the same, sharing in the responsibility of governance.

And Some General Advice

Finally, as president I learned a number of other things which I present in no particular order:

Make Governance Worthwhile. You need to behave in a way that demonstrates that spending valuable time on committees is worth the investment. The research by Birnbaum indicates that successful presidents are viewed as "influenceable." "The most important characteristic of exemplary presidents is that they are seen as continuing to respond to the faculty and willing to open themselves to faculty influence" (Birnbaum 1992, 98). If faculty regularly make reports that may be criticized by some faculty and are then ignored by the administration, the message is clear: governance is a waste of time. This leaves the field of governance open to dispirited and chronically unhappy faculty members, who may no longer be devoted to their field or their students. An important way to assess the credibility of governance at your university is to observe how many active, well regarded teachers and scholars are involved in governance.

Identify Key Faculty Members. These are faculty members whom the rest of the faculty respects, the informal leaders, and the people who seem to know everyone and who seem to speak for others. They are slow to criticize, but when they do, they reflect the concerns of other faculty members. These may be individuals who have not held formal positions of leadership, often because they did not want them, but who care about the organization. Seek out and listen carefully to these individuals, for their comments are likely to be insightful and perceptive. Do not confuse thoughtful, perceptive people who care about the university and want to give you advice on important issues, with what is almost always a small group of frustrated, isolated individuals who were at war with the previous administration and want to engage you and your administration in a similar battle.

Hold the Faculty to High Standards. Talk about excellence as it is consistent with the history and culture of your university and maintain those standards. And exemplify integrity. Each decision of consequence you make will be scrutinized for its integrity.

Communicate throughout the Organization. Informal communication goes up, down, and across the organizational chart. Be prepared to participate in that process, knowing that if you consult with key faculty members they will tell others and the information will spread. If people are not surprised about decisions because they know the facts, if they have an idea what is going on, they can accept the consequences much better.

There were times when I had to reveal bad news to my university community. By preparing key people informally, and by having established credibility before the difficult times, the community accepted it in ways that I always found gratifying, and, occasionally, even amazing. Knowing what is going to happen, even if it is bad, reduces anxiety substantially. Give people the confidence that you will keep them informed through newsletters, periodic emails, formal and informal meetings. (Do not rely too much on email, however. They are not a substitute for a face-to-face discussion.) I have always found that deciding on the frequency and detail of that process to be challenging. While people throughout the organization need to know what is going on, they do not need to drown in unnecessary detail. Talking with colleagues about the level of information they want and need from you will enable you to strike the right balance.

Create Time for Informal Interaction. Because your university is small, you can interact with faculty beyond the formal faculty leadership. Birnbaum cites as a myth the idea that a president should increase the social distance from the faculty and that, in fact, the more successful presidents were seen as having reduced the social distance between the president and the faculty (Birnbaum 1992, 34–36). You can retain your presidential role and maintain a necessary distance. Spending informal time with faculty will let you understand nuances that may be important in understanding their behavior. An informal relationship also lets you try out ideas without undercutting the formal faculty leadership. At the same time, you must always be sensitive to being perceived as especially aligned with a particular faculty faction, although it may be simply because you enjoy the company of certain individuals and have similar interests.

Pay Attention to the Work of the Faculty. The faculty do not want a bureaucrat as president; they want a leader and a colleague and they will welcome your attention. Talk to them about ideas, share articles and books. When possible, attend art openings, plays, seminars, and symposia. Sometimes you will be asked to give a welcome at an event and then you must go on to another meeting. However, on occasion you should stay and engage in the discussion, or just listen. The university is about ideas; any president too busy to engage in an exchange of ideas is a president who needs to reorder priorities. Of course, you cannot do that all of the time and the faculty understand that. However, you must make time to engage in the academic life of the community if you want to lead it. If you really believe, as you should, that their work is of great importance, let them know you believe this by your actions.

ENCOURAGE THE FACULTY IN WAYS LARGE AND SMALL. A small amount of discretionary money from your foundation can be of enormous help. Academic chairs, deans, and the academic vice president need some funds to encourage innovation and program development. You may be able to fund field trips, host and fund receptions for visiting speakers, and many other things, some of which may seem small but which convey your respect for what your faculty are doing.

ASK ABOUT THE STUDENTS. You need to understand the student body beyond their SAT scores and high school rankings. What is the faculty's perception of the students on campus? What are the concerns of the faculty about their students, and where do they see their greatest strengths? What do they think of the freshman class? The entire university, you included, has a responsibility to them, and you can understand them better through the eyes of their teachers.

NURTURE FUTURE LEADERS. Involve effective junior faculty members on committees and consult with them periodically. At colleges and universities where governance has not worked well, faculty involved in governance are often the senior faculty, some of them too focused on retirement or old grievances. Some younger faculty will be interested in the entire organization. Nurture them by providing leadership opportunities for them. Appoint them to committees and encourage your administrative colleagues to involve them as well. One of your contributions to your university should be to nurture future faculty and administration leadership.

In Chapter 1 of this book, I talked about the collegial university. This is what you are working to build or to strengthen. Robert Birnbaum said that an important characteristic of the collegial university is a reduced social distance between the faculty and the university leadership. Nowhere is that more important than in the way faculty relates to you, the president. You can retain your presidential role and a necessary distance, but the more you can build an informal network founded on trust, interaction, and the free exchange of interesting ideas, the more you will have moved your institution towards the ideal of collegiality.

Chapter 10

Students—They Are Why You're Here

> Higher education has been defined as that training which demands that a man should leave home. It means a breaking of the leading strings. It means the entrance to another atmosphere.
>
> —David Starr Jordan, President,
> Stanford University, 1902
> ("University-building," *Popular Science Monthly* 1902, 332)

Small colleges and universities pride themselves on educating the "whole person," attending to their emotional and interpersonal needs as well as to their intellectual growth. It is important that such university presidents take advantage of the smallness of their universities to ensure that the assertions in the catalogues and glossy view books are accurate. There is ample research evidence—and it is certainly consistent with my own experience—that students learn a great deal outside the classroom. It is easier to shape that experience in a small university.

In the mid-1990s I was the Deputy Chancellor at the Minnesota State Colleges and Universities before and during the time when we merged three public higher education systems into one system. Many of the technical colleges and community colleges were located in the same city, sometimes across the street from one another. Consolidating campuses in such proximity seemed to be a natural step to take as part of the merger process. I regularly met with twenty or so presidents and our meeting time was spent discussing how to handle payrolls, overlapping staffs, integrating a faculty with different traditions who might even be members of different unions.

During one of the many meetings as we dealt with complicated technical questions, one president said, "Whenever things get complicated at our college we

ask ourselves, 'What is best for the students?' This seems to help us figure out what to do."

"What is best for the students?" seems to be such an obvious question. An important question to ask regularly, and yet the question often gets lost as we focus on budget problems, board relations, work with faculty, and fundraising. We exist because of the students and for the students. Therefore, why not ask ourselves regularly how we can best be of help to them? While the question can be simply stated, it does not always make for clear, simple answers, but it is certainly a good place to start. In a small university, when you engage in those conversations, you can bring your own experience to discussions about what is best for the students if you have gotten to know a representative number of them.

You are from a different generation than your students. Do not flatter yourself that things have not changed, that you have worked with hundreds of students in the past and therefore you can understand them. Do not think you can understand the students because you have read the annual national survey of freshman attitudes each year—although I found these studies to provide a very useful first step in understanding and putting the attitudes and life goals of students at my college in a national context. The annual report by Beloit College, listing important events that freshman have not experienced because they occurred before they were born, is a regular reminder not to assume that these events are shared experiences. The writings about the Millennium Generation are helpful for generalizations but these books and articles do not replace personal knowledge. Most of what you will learn, I believe, will be reassuring. After you get beyond their short attention spans, the focus on visual learning and less on reading, their multitasking skills, and amazing computer capabilities, you will find that they are in many ways like we were as undergraduates.

Your relationship to students at a small university is quite different than at a large university. In a large institution, presidential interaction with faculty is likely to consist mostly of meetings with formal faculty leadership. This is also true with students, where presidents meet periodically with formally elected or appointed representatives of student government in regularly scheduled meetings and at times when there are problems. The situation is much different at a small place, where you can know many students by name and where you can informally solicit ideas and opinions from a more diverse group.

I have said that effective presidents see themselves at the center of the university, not simply at the top. Leadership involves having a close, personal, and intuitive understanding of the whole organization, and being at the center means you are in contact with a great many people who can help you acquire that perspective—including students. You should approach engaging students in a way that does not threaten your student services staff, who have responsibilities for student activities, housing, food service, and student government. If you regularly communicate with the student services staff about your interactions with students they will welcome your efforts, for often staff members feel their work is taken for granted, that the senior administration spends most of its time working with faculty and only turns to them when there is a problem.

Students come to their undergraduate education at a time of great intellectual and psychological promise, yet with much vulnerability. They need to be treated like whole people and you are key in making sure that this holistic approach takes place. You must see each incoming freshman class as more than a set of SAT scores and class standings whose parents, thank God, are paying for tuition and housing. You must see them as individuals whose aspirations and complications you know and feel because you have spent time with them. Further, I believe that it is important to have relationships with some of their parents, because you can learn a great deal about the concerns of your students through the eyes of their parents.

How do you get to know students, informally? Just as you work with the faculty to reduce the social distance between you and them, so must you work with the students to reduce social distance. Reducing this distance is not as difficult between us and our students as it may have been in earlier times, for the occasional awe and regular respect that our generation paid to older people in authority has eroded. Remember, however, that you are their president, not their friend, and you must act accordingly.

Reducing Social Distance

Here are some things that I did as president to reduce the social distance between me and students, and to get to know them better. My wife and I attended athletic events regularly, including occasional games at other colleges and universities. We usually sat with the parents of the student athletes and got to know them and, through them, some of the athletes. We also attended student concerts and art shows. These kinds of activities simultaneously built relations with parents and students.

When prospective students and their families visited campus, I would meet with them. I would tell the parents that if their son or daughter came to my school this was the beginning of a relationship. We were a small college and were different from other places they might visit. To demonstrate that difference I gave the parents my business card that included my email address and home phone number. I told them they could call me at any time if they had a question about a school policy, or if they thought we could help their son or daughter. After the school year started I sent a letter to the parents of new students, making the same commitment, and again including my business card. Of course, it was also essential that I reassure the academic programs, student services staff, and other offices, that I was not trying to do their jobs or undermine their appropriate authority, so I always encouraged parents to go through these offices first.

I did receive emails and phone calls from parents over the years and developed relationships with many parents that I believe were both helpful to them and also gave me insight into how the college was providing services to students. What was especially interesting to me was how many parents told me that they carried my business card with them, although few parents actually called me at home. Just knowing that there was someone they could call was comforting. Several parents told me that when they visited campus, they remembered my letter to them, sent before the academic year began.

A few of the calls were quite touching. An embarrassed mother called to say she had lost her daughter's student aid application, was working two jobs, and apologized for her disorganization. Another mother called late on a Saturday night because her son had missed a tackle in the football game earlier that day. His teammates were blaming him when the team lost the game and he was so upset that he was thinking of quitting school. A quick mailing of a new financial aid form and a call to the young man's coach quickly fixed those problems. Equally important, it reassured the parents that this was a place where their student could get help when it was needed.

I always attended and made remarks at events recognizing our honors students and I found ways to spend time with those students. As president, you must be alert for ways to act on statements about your university's commitment to excellence. Honors students, especially at less selective colleges, are gold. They challenge their fellow students, as well as faculty members. I never missed an opportunity to tell them of their importance and their contribution.

Sometimes when parents would call me about a problem that their son or daughter was having, I would handle the concern myself, whether it involved an academic problem, financial aid, or a roommate. I described myself as the occasional dean of students. You do not want to do this too often because you do not want to send a message to parents and students that they can bypass the appropriate office whenever they want. However, occasionally intervening in this way teaches you a great deal about how your college functions—more than you would learn if you were only briefed by the head of an office about their programs and services.

As part of the recruitment process, our admissions office would routinely send a post card to applicants, asking about their interests. I made sure that one of the interest areas that a student could check was fly fishing. If a student expressed an interest in fly fishing I would send a personal letter, offering to take him or her fishing, along with their parents, if they were interested. Spending a day on a trout stream with a student was a great way for me to get to know what was going on in his life.

I had discretionary money available to help students with projects. When our soccer team leadership appeared at my office needing money to go to the regional and later the national tournament because they had competed well that year, I came up with some funding, matched by student government, to help with their expenses.

It is helpful to occasionally join students for lunch or dinner. You can never be sure how it will work out, of course, for sometimes they are talkative, other times not. However, dining is a social occasion and you can often get more candid comments from students when they are having lunch with several peers than you will in your office where the setting is likely to be inhibiting.

Support the work of faculty with their students. When a guest speaker comes to campus, hold a reception with the key faculty members *and their students*. It is a way of acting on your assertion that the academic work of faculty and students is paramount. You recognize that work when you and your spouse invite them to a dinner or reception, in your home, if possible. Students and faculty are grateful for these opportunities. It is an also an opportunity for you to engage the campus community in discussions about ideas. That is why you are all at the university, after all.

There may be occasions when you will be asked to speak to a class on a topic with which you are familiar. Try to arrange your schedule to take that assignment and be well prepared. You will be evaluated by both the students and faculty by how seriously you take the assignment. There are other times when, at the invitation of the faculty member, you can sit in on classes. Take advantage of those times. Learning about the faculty and students is important to your leadership, as is demonstrating that you care about the most important activity at your university. Any time you have an opportunity to demonstrate to the campus community that you are a person with a variety of interests, especially intellectual interests, act on that opportunity. You always want to be seen, not as a stereotypical administrator, but as a fellow educator.

Finally, while your work with students is important, it is not as crucial as that of the faculty and the student affairs staff. Hire and provide support to high quality staff who are effective with students. You need to be prepared to be there when they are dealing with a difficult student, a faculty–student conflict, or a difficult parent. You must be careful about when to intervene in those situations, but if the staff know you are there to help if needed, it will be reassuring, and it is unlikely that you will become involved very often.

C H A P T E R   1 1

EXTERNAL RELATIONS

You Need Outside Help

I have always been amused by people who thought the university was some kind of cloister. That's the myth academics promote in order to keep other people away from them. I have said over and over that the university is not a sanctuary from the rest of society but a tributary to it, because the worst thing that can happen is that you begin to believe your own mythology.

—A. Bartlett Giamatti
(*A Free and Ordered Space* 1989, 1)

The Alumnus who returns for the decennial reunion finds his Alma Mater greatly changed. Usually he is inclined to think that the change has not been altogether for the better in spite of the new buildings and crowds of students. He can, in fact, name the date when his Alma Mater began to decline and to lose the real old college spirit. It was ten years ago, when was graduated what is universally conceded by all its members to be the brightest class that ever came forth from its walls.

—Edwin E. Slosson
(*Great American Universities* 1910, vii)

There is no clear and simple differentiation between the university and the larger community. Our institutions of higher education interact with and are shaped by external forces, including community and national public opinion and priorities.

Colleges and universities must recognize the concerns of the larger society and their goals must be described in ways that respond to those concerns. External relations involve working with several important groups: alumni, legislators, your local community, the news media. They are part of the environment in which our university exists and they help shape it. You are the university's most important link to those groups and you can help determine if that shaping is positive.

The last century saw the role of colleges and universities in the United States evolve from serving as "finishing schools" for the leisure classes to becoming essential contributors to a democratic society and economy. The public attitude toward our enterprise has ranged from unquestioned support at the end of World War II to increasing skepticism and scrutiny, particularly on the part of state and federal legislators.

Although you and I did not participate in the period of enormous growth and funding and enrollment immediately after World War II, we have certainly been affected by it. In fact, we are perhaps too greatly affected by that history. Administrators may misinterpret the current public mood of skepticism and conditional support for higher education as greediness and anti-intellectualism. For colleges and universities to thrive and obtain the public and private support they deserve, you must understand current public attitudes toward higher education. You must skillfully mobilize support for our enterprise, using the concepts and skills that your faculty teaches their students in government, marketing, and communications classes. As administrators we must be as analytical about ourselves as we are about the rest of society—something that does not always come easily to people who have spent their career in higher education. We must assume that we need to earn that support.

Your role is crucial. Just as there are tasks that only you can undertake inside a college or university, only you can successfully carry out certain responsibilities in governmental and community relations.

Before You Start

While the advice that follows in this and the next section repeats some of what was said in earlier chapters about working with your new constituents within your institution, now I invite you to consider these ideas in the context of external communications as well.

If You're Effective Internally, You Can Be Effective Externally. Some of the leadership skills I have already discussed that are relevant to your effectiveness internally are also relevant for your effectiveness externally. Your loosely-organized campus constituents of faculty, staff, and students often disagree among themselves about goals, priorities, and the allocation of resources. Successful leadership of such organizations requires skills in communication, listening, consensus building, and making conceptual sense out of what at times may appear to be chaos. Recognize that these are political skills and, having already learned to apply them internally, you can be sure that they will be equally invaluable in your work off campus.

Recognize also that your internal effectiveness is part of a good advocacy strategy. Earlier, I gave the example of the legislator who heard good things about the college where I was president from one of his relatives who happened to be on the staff at this college. The relative's credibility about the new momentum at the college caused the legislator to help the college on our behalf, unsolicited. Letting others speak for you is often more important than speaking yourself, for it appears to be more objective. Institutional advancement staff members are a part of that informal network. They may have been at the institution much longer than you have been. They are likely to be graduates or to have been employed in the community. As such, they can be very useful, ensuring that your messages, accurate ones, are included in the community conversation.

COMPELLING VISION AND GOALS. The degree to which legislators, alumni, donors, and others support a specific school, college, or university greatly depends on how well you have articulated a vision for your institution. It must be a set of goals that makes sense to community members, alumni, donors, and legislators. The goals must be consistent with their view of reality and address issues they believe important.

TRANSLATION AND STORYTELLING. It must be noted, however, that a stirring vision and set of goals are not enough. Earlier, I talked about the effective president as one who is both deeply inside the culture of his or her university, and is also outside it, so that the president can play the important role of translator. Your message that works well internally, typically couched in the specialized language of higher education, must be decoded when you are interacting externally. Indeed, you must step back even further, recognizing that the most basic assumptions that you and your higher education colleagues share are not necessarily assumptions shared by the people with whom you are conversing.

Making the message understandable is not always easy. Universities, like other specialized activities, have their own language. You must decode this language into words and terms that the public can understand. For example, the business community prides itself on having a "bottom line" that can provide clear indicators on how they are doing on a regular basis. Our "product" is teaching and learning and to a large degree we decide what our students should learn. While students act like customers on occasion, they are not. Businesses are also more hierarchical and their staff don't have tenure. As an educator, you must regularly acknowledge and address these differences in speeches, legislative meetings, and governing board meetings. While this can be a challenge, remind yourself that American higher education is the envy of the world. You are an educator and this is one of your assignments.

Successful Communications

A successful government and community relations program features the following elements.

Effective Communication. I have already emphasized the need for clear and understandable goals. Do not assume the faculty, staff, and students—much less external constituents—remember or perhaps even understand these goals. They must be repeated in internal newsletters, speeches, and alumni publications, they must be grounded in things that matter to people and they must be clear. The best way for you to determine if you are communicating effectively is to review the comments you made in newsletters, alumni publications, speeches, and internal memos for the past year. Do they address important goals of the organization, or are they primarily about management issues? A president communicating mostly about changes in parking regulations, snow removal, and building management is not going to inspire donations from alumni or legislative appropriations.

Ability to Listen. Communication goes both ways. Most people who want to talk to you about your university care about it, often deeply. In fact, the commitment of community members or alumni to their college or university is often for life. These individuals may be seeking confirmation that the president and members of the advancement team—some of whom probably came from somewhere else—are as committed. They want to tell you about their experiences, good and bad, and about the unique history of the place they love. Get a dozen people who know about the college or university together and ask them to tell you about their university. Confine your role to asking questions and soliciting more information. The results will be helpful and can be surprising. The participants also will be pleased they were asked for their insights and advice. Retired faculty and staff who remain in the community often can offer a different perspective about their university. They have absorbed the rhythms and values of the community where they have lived for many years and can provide great insights.

At a university with a troubled history of community and alumni relations, new presidents and institutional advancement staff members may interpret the deep unhappiness and occasional bitterness as permanent disillusionment with the organization. This would be a mistake. Most alumni, legislators, and community members are prepared to support the university again. As in all relationships, however, they must be convinced that things will be different and that they will be listened to. It takes special patience on the part of the president and the advancement staff to repair these relationships, but it is worth the time. Often, supporters will renew their support with greater enthusiasm than ever, wanting to make up for the lost time and opportunities.

ABILITY TO DEVELOP ALLIES. You may feel beleaguered and alone when you are dealing with a problem or trying to achieve a goal, but you are not alone. People are prepared to help if you seek their help and will be flattered that you asked. Community leaders have an important stake in your institution's success. Successful alumni are proud of their institution. Newspaper editors are key leaders, particularly in smaller communities. Properly informed, and not just during difficult times, they can inform and shape public opinion.

There are allies off campus who are constituents of specific programs and they can help as well. Athletic boosters, agribusiness leaders, accountants, media professionals, and others who graduated from your institution can be enormously helpful. Some of them have relationships with legislators and donors and more credibility in those relationships than you will ever have. For this reason, when you need help, remember your program-specific friends as well as those who care more generally about the welfare of your college.

A PROGRAM BUILT ON STRENGTH. One of your important jobs is identifying the strengths and history of your college when you are building your external relations as much as when you are developing your internal goals. The people you will be asking for help understand that history and they want you to honor it. It is why they remain attached to the place.

Vartan Gregorian, president of the Carnegie Corporation and former president of Brown University, served as president of the New York Public Library in the 1980s. He said that he carefully reflected on the history and character of New York City before choosing goals for the library. He realized that the people of New York City liked things that were big and ambitious, consistent with the history of that city. He chose a fund-raising goal for the library that some thought was far too ambitious for what seemed to be a declining institution. He believes he was successful because he chose a goal that was congruent with the story that New Yorkers tell about their city and themselves and he challenged the city to live up to that history.

STEPS TO TAKE

Here is very specific advice about things to remember to do in leading a successful program of governmental and community relations.

THANK HELPERS. This may seem obvious. Institutional leaders believe their projects are so important and their merits so obvious, that they sometimes forget to thank those who have helped them accomplish their goal. However, legislators need to be thanked because they stand for election every few years and you want them to be friendly to you in their next term. Alumni and others supporters are enormously flattered by private and public expressions of thanks from their college or university, particularly when expressed by the president; your title carries great respect with them.

WORK WITH PEOPLE, BEYOND THE OBVIOUS LEADERS. Younger, junior individuals may have more time to devote to your cause than do senior people. Also, these groups are quite heterogeneous. Older business leaders, with established companies, may have a very different attitude about their university than do younger entrepreneurs with small, start-up companies. In addition, annual donors can become major donors later in their lives. Backbenchers in the legislature become leaders. Newspaper reporters become editors. Junior managers become senior managers.

DON'T WHINE. People want to work for something important. They want to help make your institution better, not just fix problems. They want to be a part of something bigger than themselves. Convey a vision for your college or university with which they can identify. Focus on opportunities, not problems.

START LOCALLY. When people consider running for public office, they first seek support from their friends and then work to expand their base. In the same way, spend time with local community members, alumni, and legislators, asking them to help shape your ideas. Your plans will probably be stronger as a result, and your public relations will certainly be stronger. If the people who are close to the university can understand your idea, you may be able to explain it to people who are not as close or as involved. If these people tell you that your proposal is not a good one, listen to them—maybe it isn't!

Do Not Burn Bridges. It has been said that in politics there are no permanent friends and no permanent enemies. While some people view this statement cynically, it simply means that support will come from one source for a particular project and from another source for a different proposal. A donor or legislator who does not support your proposal may be there the next time you ask. Be certain to behave in a way that allows you to approach that person the next time. Do not assume that people who do not agree with you are badly motivated or will always disagree.

Keep in Touch. Seeking help from community members, legislators, and donors involves building relationships. In any relationship, no one likes to be approached only when they are needed. They like to know what is going on at their university. Community leaders, donors, and legislators appreciate being involved at times when they are not being asked for direct assistance.

This communication should be formal as well as informal. When I was president, I was a member of the local "Mayors and Managers" group, an informal collection of city and county officials who met regularly to share issues and concerns. We also had a President's Advisory Council composed of key citizens in our area whom I kept informed about college programs and problems and who provided advice on those issues. Membership in your chamber of commerce, your service club, or other groups is also important.

Involve Others. Of course there are certain roles that only you or people with certain administrative roles can perform. But there are many others within your college or university who can help. When you attend your next alumni function, listen carefully. Your graduates will talk not only about the university in general, but will also talk about faculty members who shaped their lives and whom they will never forget. Try to find ways for these faculty members to participate in your external relations campaign. I often said to the faculty that I thought I was fairly effective in describing the college and its work in my meetings with alumni. However, when faculty talk with the same people they are not simply describing what others are doing, but what *they* are doing. Because teaching is viewed as central to the mission of the university, they *are* the university to those with whom they meet.

I began this chapter by noting that competition for public and private funds and community support is intense and that unquestioning allegiance to higher education can no longer be assumed. Public universities are inevitably competing for public dollars with public school education, the correctional system, and other state agencies. The share of the budget devoted to public higher education has declined in virtually every state in the nation during the last twenty years. Private colleges and universities compete for students and private contributions, often struggling to keep their tuition within reach of their prospective students.

A college education, once rare, has been earned by more than 25% of the adult population of our country. Universal access to higher education, the dream of many who preceded us in our work, has nearly been achieved. We have been successful. However, with that success, the awe with which a college degree was once regarded has diminished. As a result, some university administrators have become disheartened as they compete for funding. We should not be. The clear evidence is that college and university attendance is valued highly by the American public. Indeed, the great question among the public about higher education is not whether their sons and daughters *should* attend college, but whether they can afford it. There continues to be much support for our work, both politically and financially. However, we cannot assume that support will be there for every project we think worthy. We must communicate clearly about those important ideas and projects. We must listen to what our critics, especially our friendly critics, have to say when they offer us suggestions on improving our enterprise.

I know that some presidents and others in higher education may find this work slightly distasteful and "political." It is true that the public universities must approach elected officials and donors for our appropriations and our private contributions. The manner in which this is done varies considerably from state to state and you must learn and be sensitive to those traditions. In this we are like many other causes. However, our traditions and causes are unique. Among these traditions, one of the most important is that higher education is protected from the daily political forces that press upon other organizations. If this tradition is to be honored by those who provide resources to us, our integrity, reflected in our relations with the public, community members, alumni, legislators, and governing boards must be impeccable.

It is most important that we behave in ways that are consistent with what we say we believe and that we be timely and accurate in our communications. Because our product is ideas, we must be persuasive, but our persuasion must be based upon solid facts. If we act just like another lobbying group or funding-raising cause, we do great harm to our universities.

In much of our promotion of higher education, we are harvesting the work of those who preceded us. Donors are more likely to give if they see their college or university going in a good direction, one consistent with its history and tradition. They give because of faculty and staff who worked with them—individuals who, for the most part, made those contributions before we arrived. We must contribute to and perpetuate that legacy.

C H A P T E R   1 2

How to Get the Best People

Personnel Searches

> By and large, executives make poor promotion and staffing deci-
> sions. By all accounts, their batting average is no better than
> .333: at most one-third of such decisions turn out right,
> one-third are minimally effective, and one-third are outright
> failures.
>
> —Peter Drucker
> (*The Essential Drucker* 2001, 127)

Searches represent perhaps the most challenging task for faculty and staff committees, involving at their best, a continuing relationship with the president.
Shared governance, which is your goal, requires conversation, not separation of
powers, to meet your common goal of identifying the best candidate for your college.

The Challenge

Choosing effective colleagues is one of your most important jobs. In higher education we have delegated much of this difficult task to faculty and staff—amateurs,
at least in personnel selection. Members of search committees for senior administrators often do not have a good understanding of what the job involves and, as a
result, focus on issues such as sensitivity to the faculty role on the part of the candidates. This is important, but is not the most important skill of a cabinet member.

You inherited an organizational culture that probably defines how searches
are done. It is important that you carefully review these traditions, and if the process does not identify the best candidates, or if it dilutes your important authority

to make personnel decisions, you must change them, tradition aside. Again, keep in mind that if you do make changes, it is essential to communicate why you are doing so, what the principles are that led to your decisions.

The purpose of a search committee is to identify the best candidates for the position. I have found two situations especially challenging. The first is the search committee whose members feel that they have "rights" to represent a particular perspective or faction on campus. This search committee works more like a group of United Nations delegates than a group of disparate people working together to achieve a common purpose. The second is the search committee that is excessively burdened by procedure. Committee members are so intent on adhering to the correct process, avoiding lawsuits by treating every candidate in identical fashion, and making sure that every committee member can attend each meeting, that they fail to discern the best candidates in the thicket of paperwork and process.

In both cases the result may be a list of finalists who are "safe" and who will not be likely to make significant changes at the university. Then you, as president, can only make your final decision from among uninspiring candidates. Rather than continuous consultation and communication, there is too often a division of labor in which committee members jealously guard their prerogatives to identify the finalists. The committee retreats behind a cloak of confidentiality and their work takes place in a black box.

As a college president, and more recently as a consultant on searches, I have found that early discussion with the committee about the goals of the search and the importance of the role of the committee can help establish a relationship in which we are in agreement on the goals and we work as a team. It is another occasion to remind them of what you should have already informed them in writing, that the candidate list you receive should be unranked. Also, it is a time to talk about the qualifications needed for the position as well as the skills the university needs. This may be the only occasion when they will be reminded of the perspective of the president.

What to Look For

The person chosen should, of course, be technically competent and have good work habits and ethics. Importantly, candidates should *not* want to come to your college to do exactly what they did in their previous job. You need people who are capable of adapting their skills and applying them to the new position. Never confuse experience with competence. Just because someone has done a job for a long time does not mean it has been done well. Many people make the same mistakes year after year in their work. Although talent and experience are important, and the ideal candidate has both, I choose talent over experience if I have to make that choice.

To achieve the goal, the position description and ad must be written carefully and you should write or at least carefully approve it before it goes to the committee. The organization must really understand what it is looking for; the search must be expeditiously conducted, references carefully checked, and the insights of each person who met with the candidate should be solicited. It should be clear from the start of the search that you will make the final decision.

GETTING READY TO SEARCH

The Job Announcement

The search process begins with the posting of the job notice. Ads should be clear about experience and preparation, the qualities sought, the required and the preferred qualifications. Do not write the ad so broadly that you get large numbers of candidates who are not right for the position. At the same time, do not write it so narrowly that you get too few candidates. Be careful not to require too many years of experience. If you do, you will only have applicants for whom the position will be a lateral transfer from their current university and you will have excluded some talented, less experienced applicants.

I prefer to leave deadlines open so that later applicants get full consideration although, of course, you must be clear about the general time frame—you can't wait forever. The ad can read, "The committee will begin reviewing applications on <insert date>, and will continue that review until a suitable candidate is identified." Alternative wording is, "review will continue until a pool of finalists is identified." The best candidates often apply toward the end of the search. You do not want to disqualify an applicant because they applied one day after an artificial deadline.

The Committee Members

The invitation to serve should be in writing and the committee should have their initial meeting with you to receive their charge. Composition of the committee is crucial and will reflect the history of such committees at your university, as well as your interest in getting people who can find the best candidates. It is especially important that the committee not include too many people who report to one another, or too many members who will be a peer or report to the chosen candidate. A credible search committee needs to include representatives from throughout the university. However, you must take great care in making sure that a faculty, staff, or student group that might make nominations does not tie your hands.

You should identify the committee chair in the letter that provides the charge to the committee. Do not leave that important responsibility to the committee. Otherwise, the committee will be forced to select a chair at its first meeting, before they have gotten to know one another. Also, it introduces another uncertainty in a process that already has an uncertain outcome.

Try to find a chair who is effective at building consensus, comfortable with conflict and dealing with members who have their own agendas. Many things can, and often do, go wrong during a search. There are reasons why search and screening committees have been called "shirk and scream" and "search and destroy." Finally, you should be confident that the chair is someone who recognizes that search committees tend to be conservative, seeking people who maintain the status quo, and can make at least a conscientious effort to run the search in a way that the strongest, forward-looking candidates are recommended.

When you give the charge to the committee, request that they not only discuss the qualifications of the candidates, but their assessment of how they might fit into the organization. Also, be sure to talk about the importance of honoring the confidentiality of the candidates. This is always important, but of greater significance when there are internal candidates for the position. The laws and procedures vary among states in the public sector and among private colleges and universities, but whatever the exact laws and protocols that guide your search, you must follow its spirit, as well.

It is very important to emphasize that you seek three to five *unranked* candidates, so that you can make the decision. You can specify a minimum number of candidates, but do not specify an *exact* number of candidates. Suppose, for example, you require four names; the committee may feel obliged to include a weak candidate just to meet your requirement.

REVIEWING APPLICATIONS

The committee (and ultimately, of course, you) should look for well-written letters that are concise and reflect an understanding of the position. Look for letters that are not generic, that respond directly to the requirements listed in the ad —the person may be applying for many positions using the same letter.

Look for gaps in the résumé, such as missing years in the chronology of job experience. This could reflect periods of unemployment—not necessarily a reason to reject someone, but clearly something that should be addressed with the candidate. When there is doubt about a particular candidate, it is often a good idea to keep him or her in contention until the committee obtains more information. Too often committees spend inordinate amounts of time differentiating among candidates about whom they know very little. If, for example, there are fifty applications, and the committee can easily reduce the list to fifteen serious candidates, it should not waste time trying to get the list smaller before taking additional steps—there is probably not enough information to make informed decisions. The committee can have telephone or video interviews or make reference calls before narrowing a list to the finalists. Never create a list of finalists from resumes and job applications alone.

Some committee members develop point systems to evaluate the candidates. This creates a false sense of precision, suggesting an explicit understanding and agreement of the importance of each of the responsibilities of the position—and the candidate's preparation—when in fact those rarely exist. Do not get bogged down over some very specific aspect of the candidate's application. Committee members can become entangled in minute and detailed discussions. If they knew more about the candidates, those specifics would often be virtually meaningless. The goal is for the committee to have a candid discussion of candidate qualifications.

The committee may find conference calls helpful as they determine the list of semi-finalists. Conference calls are inexpensive and the committee can learn a lot about the candidates. Then the committee can meet with you after the conference calls and provide names and résumés of the semi-finalists to you. This makes the search process more transparent and less like the secret deliberations of the Supreme Court, which can only be good for your university.

You can then make calls to the semi-finalists, talking about the position and the salary range. This will almost certainly reduce the list, as some candidates will have already taken jobs; some do so badly in the discussion that they do not warrant further consideration; some reveal aspects of their current employment situation that suggests they are in serious trouble with their employer (which is not necessarily a disqualifier, but you should certainly take it as a warning sign); some have provided only a phone number because they are not employed, despite what their resume says; and others may have salary expectations that are clearly beyond what is possible. Remember, not only are you evaluating the candidates, but also the candidates are evaluating you and the institution. It should be a conversation to benefit both parties. You then report your perceptions to the committee.

By receiving the list of semi-finalists from the entire committee, then making calls, then reporting back to the entire committee, you develop or deepen a relationship of trust between you and the committee members. Not only does this increase teamwork at your college, but it also contributes information to the campus gossip that you are someone who shoulders the workload and treats colleagues with respect.

FURTHER CHECKING OF QUALIFICATIONS

Never check references of a candidate without their approval. Because you will offer the job to a single candidate from among many candidates, you have an obligation to not damage the careers of any of the other applicants. When the initial reference checks and the first telephone interview are completed, there are doubtless questions that remain and can be explored more fully in a second interview. Always look for candidates who have been promoted within their own institution; they impressed people who know them very well. I am wary of candidates who have held many jobs and moved after two or three years in each position. Also, look for candidates with "holes" in their resumes, and people who claimed to be consulting while they are a candidate for your position. They are likely to have been fired from their previous position. Administrators report to someone and also have peers and subordinates. Try to learn how the candidates relate to those individuals. It is not uncommon to hire someone who is very responsive to you, but is widely disliked by staff members.

Do not bring a candidate to campus without having first checked references, going beyond the five or so they have provided, and without having interviewed the candidate by phone or video conference, if possible. Never bring a candidate to campus without the candidate having a clear understanding of the salary you can offer.

INTERVIEWING CANDIDATES

I always remind search committees that interviews, while important, are often misleading. The goal is not to find the candidate who interviews best, but someone who knows what to do on the job on their first Monday morning of work. It is also important for you and committee members to understand the unreliability of interviews. The research makes clear that we all make up our minds very quickly about people and do so with very little information (Myers 2002, 187–197; Gladwell 2000b). Those impressions are often inaccurate. One way to reduce that distorting effect is for a number of people to talk to the candidate and then share their impressions—before they develop a strong consensus that may lose the insights of some of the interviewers.

Research on interview effectiveness indicates that asking people specific questions about how they have handled situations in their current and previous employment are most helpful (Campion, Palmer, and Campion 1997). Make certain that the questions cover all important aspects of the position description and that there is agreement on what constitutes a good answer to the questions. Questions of the candidate about prospective issues are more a test of their creativity than how they would actually do the job. The standard interview questions about preparation and interest in the job are fine for starters. If the candidate cannot answer these questions, you have to wonder about their preparation for the interview as well as the position.

As you progress, there is nothing wrong with helping the candidate relax. This is not simply a stress test. However, there should be thorough and challenging questions for the candidate as well. Here are some typical questions for the interview:

- What work experiences have prepared you for this position?
- Could you describe how you see this position and the kind of work you will be doing each day? (You only want people who can learn on the job and understand that they will not be doing their former job in a new location.)
- Describe a few successes you've had. How were they accomplished? (You want to notice whether the candidates claims accomplishments heroically and all alone, or by involving others and giving them credit.)
- Describe a difficult assignment you had to undertake that did not necessarily result in great success. What did you learn from that experience? (Understanding and working with ambiguity is essential for any senior position. Also, defensiveness and blaming others is important to identify, as well as good analytical skills and judgment.)
- I would like to describe a hypothetical challenge you might face. Could you describe how you would approach this situation? Who

would you talk with, what information would you need, what would be the most important factors you would consider?

- Let's think about the possibility that you are in this position for three years. What will people at the university be saying about you and your contribution to the university?

Additional questions that can be helpful:

- What is different about the job you are applying for and the job you have now? What is similar? What would you need to do differently? What would you need to learn? (Too often, when people get a new position, with more authority, their response is to work harder, rather than differently.)

- Describe a conflict with a colleague, or former colleague. How did you handle it? What would that person say about you if we called that person?

- We have provided you information about our organization (assuming this is true—and it should certainly be true by the time of even a phone interview). What are your preliminary thoughts about our university based on this information? (The idea here is to determine that they have given some real thought to the job and how they approach new situations. Also, it is a way to help determine if they believe they have all of the answers, when they obviously have little information to have firm ideas about many important matters involving the university.)

- Most positions could be broken down into about five parts. None of us gets a perfect score in each of those areas. For example, I always have to work harder at <provide personal example> and I keep working on that area. What are some things that you are working on? (Simply asking the candidate about his or her strengths and weaknesses question is usually not productive because it is too broad and threatening. Structuring the question in such a way makes it less daunting—and more revealing.)

- If you were offered this position and accepted it, how would you expect to have your areas of responsibility functioning and contributing to the university after you had been on the job for a year?

While the candidate is on campus, try to identify issues that could cause a problem in what seems like a smooth hiring process. These can include the candidate's interest in receiving tenure or a position for the spouse at the university or in the community. (I have been surprised to receive calls from candidates who appeared eager to accept the position but then told me that their spouse would not move! Although we can hope they would have discussed this issue before they came to the interview, family relationships are complicated and you can never be certain.) Some candidates seem to find it interesting or flattering to fly around the country being interviewed for jobs they have no intention of taking. Others are so confident of their abilities they believe they can negotiate for a salary $10,000, even $20,000 higher than what you can offer.

It can be useful for some interviews to be conducted by two people. This gives the interviewers better opportunity to observe and ask follow-up questions, and the teamwork approach eliminates pressure on a single interviewer to keep the conversation going while also thinking of the next question.

Often candidate visits are heavily structured, totally unlike the reality the candidate will face on the job, if it were offered. While the research demonstrates that structured questions are the most revealing in an interview situation, it is helpful to create opportunities for leisurely conversations, so that you can get to know the candidate well. A dinner with you and your spouse or a senior colleague can provide that opportunity.

As the interview progresses, probably over a two-day period, it is important to allow time for the interviewers to gather and compare notes and questions. Sometimes the questions concern attitudes and sometimes the questions concern job experience. A meeting allows them to formulate questions for the candidate before he or she leaves town. The appointing authority should have the final interview with the candidate, posing the questions or probing issue areas that arose during the meeting of the interview committee.

If the candidate has made a good impression, you might ask for additional names of people that you or the committee can call to further discuss their questions. You can also ask permission to contact people whom the candidate has *not* identified as references. This must be done carefully. It is not unusual that candidates do not want their boss called unless they are about to receive a job offer, for example. In other cases, the boss may be quite accepting of the fact that the person is looking for a promotion and may want to be helpful. Candidates should be treated with care and respect. You have a professional responsibility to do no harm to the career of any of the candidates.

AFTER THE INTERVIEW

Meet with the committee and request the views about the candidates from *each person in the room*. Often the quietest person on the committee will have the most insight into the candidates. In *The Wisdom of Crowds*, James Surowiecki reports that non-expert individuals who provide their opinions before their peers influence them, can be very insightful when those opinions are averaged (Surowiecki 2004). The other advantage of meeting with the committee and getting the opinions of each of the committee members is that it reduces the likelihood that the committee will informally rank the candidates.

As issues are identified about the candidates, you can follow up by calling references a second time and asking the questions that have developed during the interviews. For particularly important appointments I have found that having someone visit the candidate's campus and talking with colleagues directly can be very useful. You can ask the candidate to arrange the meetings by writing a carefully composed letter that the candidate can share with his or her colleagues when setting up the meetings. It would be ideal that you, or your representative, meet with the person to whom the candidate reports, peers of the candidate, and people who report to the candidate. There is usually a higher level of candor when you are physically in the office of the person you are interviewing.

MAKING THE OFFER

It is important that you have already begun general discussions with all of the finalists about salary, living in the community, and possible employment for spouses so that possible problems have been identified prior to this last stage. When you make the offer, you should:

- State terms and conditions clearly, in writing.
- Make no promises you can't deliver on, such as tenure, spouse appointment.
- Write a letter of appointment with the assumption that it may become public, however unlikely that may be.

Request a specific date by which the candidate must respond. This is important because candidates are typically in more than one search. If they are delaying responding to you because they want to hear from another university, you may extend slightly the deadline, but you deserve to know the facts. You may need to go to another candidate yourself, someone you do not want to lose.

How & Why Presidents Fail

Crises, Causes, & Cures

[I] had left the presidency of the university as I had entered it:
"fired with enthusiasm;" my own on the way in, that of certain
others on my way out.

—Clark Kerr
(*The Gold and the Blue* 2001, 309)

It was an absolute, complete shock.

It was unbelievable, even though my chair had been hinting and
even warning me, it was still a terrible shock.

—Presidents' comments on being fired
(Penson, *Flashpoints of "Troubled" Presidencies* n.d., 1)

Presidents come to their new jobs with great enthusiasm and optimism. These
sentiments are shared by the board that hired you as well as the faculty and staff
who anticipate your arrival, some of whom were involved in your selection. Some
will hope that you will do as well as your predecessor. More typically, your constituents hope you will do well at all of the things your predecessor did well, and
will improve on what that individual did not do so well. An impossible assignment? No, but a difficult one. Often those hopes are dashed and expectations are
lowered within a matter of months. It is then said that "the honeymoon is
over"—the honeymoon being a sort of finite pile of chits that are provided to the
new president which are used up rather quickly, before reality sets in.

When athletes consult with sports psychologists about how to improve
their performance, perhaps the most important advice they receive is to focus on

success. They are asked to envision hitting the ball or making the basket, not to *avoid missing*. They must picture themselves being successful. In a close game, good shooters want the ball because they are confident they can score. I have taken that approach in this book. I have described ways to understand your organization and, based on that understanding, behave in ways that help ensure success. However, it is also important to be able to detect early what you might be doing wrong so you can take corrective steps before you get too far off track.

This chapter is written with the reminder that earlier in this book I described leadership as a craft. Craftspeople must adhere to certain techniques and principles, but they do their work differently, just as you will. It is the principles that I focus on here and how violation of those principles may get you into trouble.

I first cite the kind of troubles presidents get into, then some causes of those troubles, and, finally, steps to take to correct them (or, even better, prevent them from occurring). You will recognize many of the examples and you may experience some of them. Let me be clear that experiencing these or other problems does not mean you will fail in your job. Not identifying and correcting them, however, will certainly increase your likelihood of failure. I cite these examples before I discuss the principles for avoiding them in order to get your attention. If you have not yourself experienced these problems, you probably know presidents who have, and you have certainly read about others in the *Chronicle of Higher Education*. They range from big things to small things—but be attentive to the small things, for they can become serious if you do not handle them carefully.

PROBLEMS

CONFLICTING EXPECTATIONS OF IMPORTANT CONSTITUENTS. Consider the situation of a new president who is taken aside by several board members and told that his university is in desperate shape and that he would have board support for taking drastic measures. The faculty may not perceive, or understand, the extent of those problems, or might not believe that major changes are needed. Expectations placed upon the president often vary greatly among constituent groups, especially faculty and board members. Presidents become caught in those different perceptions of their jobs and feel they have nowhere to turn and can make no one happy.

PERSONNEL PROBLEMS. You may inherit a difficult senior staff member who has personal problems, has offended many on campus, wanted your job and did not get it, has become very fixed in his or her approach to the job, or expects the relationship with you will be the same as it was with the previous president. You will be tempted to fire that individual and maybe you should. Presidents are also tempted to demonstrate who is the boss, that they are now in charge, and that they require loyalty and competence—all essential for a well-functioning team. However, these decisions made early and without quiet consultation can cause problems which will distract you from other important matters and, in the worst case, from which you may never recover.

FINANCIAL PROBLEMS. Presidents often do not have an extensive background in finance and are apt to spend much of their time the first six months on external relations and getting to know people on campus. We naturally do the things we are most comfortable with, but postponing addressing the budget is dangerous. Many presidents have told me of their shock at discovering early on in their new job that they are facing significant financial problems and possible layoffs. Balancing budgets is hard work and your predecessor, perhaps fatigued, may have become lax about making tough decisions.

ADDING AND DROPPING ACADEMIC PROGRAMS. It is not uncommon for universities to avoid addressing declining enrollment in academic programs or to avoid responding to student interests in new academic majors. The declining program is staffed by people who are part of the campus community, people with families needing jobs. A new program possibility may be a tantalizing and sound idea but is an abstraction without local advocates because the program does not yet have students or faculty. A new president examines the university budget, sees some programs financially supporting others, and sees the potential for new student enrollments with the addition of new programs. He or she quickly proclaims that these issues need to be addressed at once and is quickly embroiled in meetings, phone calls, and letters from unhappy parents, students, alumni, and affected faculty.

FACULTY TENURE AND RETENTION DECISIONS. These decisions invariably involve faculty, as they should. The extent of that involvement varies fairly widely from university to university, but these decisions lie at the heart of faculty governance. Presidents have denied or granted tenure or retention of faculty members—against the recommendation of faculty committees—and then have spent a year or more meeting with faculty members and board members, sometimes even appearing in court to explain and defend those decisions.

ATHLETIC PROGRAMS. Presidents often come to their jobs with little understanding of athletic administration and sometimes, little understanding of athletic competition. They inherit programs with losing records, financial problems, and controversial coaches, some of whom have developed more personal support than a new president could hope to have. Board members, parents of athletes, and alumni are very happy to give advice about how to handle any of these situations.

Miscellaneous Troubles. These are small, but often painful and sometimes fatal problems that you can experience, especially early in the job. They are kinds of things that will keep you awake at night, will cause you to wonder how you ever got into them, and can cause you to forget what you started out the week trying to accomplish.

- Renovating the President's House. The house needs work, it has been neglected, the decorating is awful, it is like living in an aquarium, and you don't even get to build equity for your next home. Others on campus and the community may not see it that way. Your house is certainly a lot bigger and nicer than theirs and they have to make house payments and pay utilities!

- Interacting with the Media. The reporter caught you in the middle of a meeting; you did not want to talk about the issue because you had not yet made a decision. In addition, the problem has been described in such a convoluted way, that there is nothing you can say that will make sense. The report may appear in the student newspaper, whose editor has a deep devotion to the first amendment and is cynical about administrators. You make a remark read by everyone on campus and the community and eventually by board members, and you spend a painful amount of time explaining what you meant.

- Offending Alumni. Alumni have ideas about how things should be done, maybe because they have donated money or might donate money in the future. And they have a much longer association with their university than you have had, or will ever have. You have dinner with an important alumnus and describe lots of campus problems. The alumnus makes suggestions that you don't follow and you have a strained relationship with a person important to the campus. And that alum knows lots of other important people as well.

- Violating Symbols. How could anyone get so worked up over a mascot or tearing down that old, outmoded building on campus? What may seem to you, the newcomer, to be a strange costume worn by a student at athletic events, offensive to some and beloved by others, or an eyesore on campus, may be an important icon to the students and alumni.

Causes

These issues occur for reasons that are not all of your making, although it may seem that way to your critics. Although any president can experience problems, some presidents seem to have them in bunches. They get out of one jam, with some pain and loss of credibility, but in a recoverable way, only to have another problem arise. Our behavior is not random. Many of these patterns are positive, resulting in strong, lasting trusting relationships and confidence on the part of others about our reliability, while others can cause problems.

Other behavior traits cause difficulty in our new jobs. We probably do not know about these traits; they might not have affected many people, or others did not bring them to our attention. However, people are watching and learning about them, and you had better pay attention to them as well. What are some of these traits? Some of these are invariably involved when problems occur, especially when they persist.

MAKING BIG DECISIONS BEFORE YOU KNOW THE ORGANIZATION. As they said in the musical *The Music Man*, you have to know the territory. The natural tendency is to want to take command and demonstrate that you are in charge. The worst advice I ever got was from a former administrator who recommended, shortly after I became president, that I seek an opportunity to make a clear, firm, and somewhat controversial decision to demonstrate that I was the boss. My predecessors had done just that, shortening their effectiveness and tenure in office. The people at my new college knew I had the authority; they wanted some assurance that I could exercise it wisely.

MAKING EXCESSIVE PROMISES. Presidents come into their new positions with high expectations, sometimes unrealistic ones. They make promises they cannot keep. Often those commitments are to raise large amounts of money. I know of a president who came to a small, under-funded university, with a small enrollment and modest alumni base, who announced that he would raise $75 million. He could, of course, not come close to that goal.

NOT COMMUNICATING. People are not thinking about what you are thinking about, at least not as deeply or as often. Communication and explanations are crucial to doing your job.

SPENDING ALL DAY IN THE OFFICE. It is comforting in there, surrounded by loyal assistants and having people of your choosing come to see you at your convenience. It is also dangerous and will guarantee that you do not get all of the information you need to make important decisions.

Talking Only to People Who Agree with You. This is also quite comforting. You can agree that the people who are criticizing you are misguided, or, even worse, badly motivated. You can construct heroic, Churchillian views of yourself as standing firmly in the face of problems and criticism.

Blaming Others. Surely, there are others to blame. People whom you would think should know better, including faculty, staff, and board members, can have a startlingly limited or inaccurate view of your job, including the extent of your authority and your real choices for a decision.

Assuming Your Critics Are Few. Although you have persistent critics, you are sure that you have broad support. It's equally unfortunate to assume the opposite. You need to assess how widespread disagreements with your policies really are and whether critics truly speak for people other than themselves.

Continuing To Do What You've Done. The first thing to do when you are in a hole is to stop digging. A common tendency is to simply work harder, but in the same way on the same problems, making things worse.

Cures

You may not have caused all of the problems, but you do have to deal with them. And you certainly want to avoid causing problems in the future. However, your response to a problem at hand can address it or worsen it. Some of these ideas will be familiar, because I discussed them in Chapter 7 when I was talking about your first year. However, the themes are important enough to be repeated here.

Move Carefully. Before you make big decisions, you need to learn about the organization, its culture, who is tolerated and who is beloved, even for their eccentricities. You can learn those things only by observing, talking, and listening to people inside and out the organization. You need to learn which problems are real.

On private decisions, such as personnel decisions, you need to find a handful of trustworthy people to talk with to get a broad perspective about the individual involved, the strengths and weaknesses of the person. An individual who has been at your university for a while may have made some tough decisions and acquired some critics. Be careful to allow for this and get specific information about what they have done that might have caused people to be unhappy. Also, there are people who are loved or at least accepted, even with their quirks and eccentricities. Presidents are sometimes startled to learn that a person they have let go has more support than they imagined. Early, quick decisions, without consultation, while you are still being carefully scrutinized can cause problems from which you might not recover.

COMMUNICATE. As you are consulting, you need to communicate your concerns, interests, and plans. Never assume that what is on your mind is on the mind of the people with whom you are working, especially the people who are not senior administrators. You may have a great many details on a subject that others will know very little about. You must carefully create a context for them and then explain it in a way they can understand. Making complicated issues understandable is a gift that comes more easily to some than others. Keep working on it. Before you make public remarks or send out an important memo, try it out on a couple of other people whose judgment you trust, who will be candid with you. When you get a response to your communication, incorporate those concerns and questions into your next communication.

Always remember that what seems to you to be minor and perhaps private messages are likely to be conveyed to others at the university. People are watching and listening.

DELEGATE. You do not need to rush in and decide every issue. In fact, rushing in to resolve an issue may *create* a crisis where none existed before. Save yourself for important issues, the real crises, where your leadership will be needed so that when you do intervene you will be credible. When you speak out on an issue to the entire campus community, you want them to listen. No one is listened to if they are talking all of the time. Franklin D. Roosevelt is still remembered for his fireside chats. In over twelve years, he only made slightly over thirty of them, even though he led our country through the Great Depression and World War II, two of the biggest crises in our history.

FOCUS ON MEANING. You are probably good at accumulating and remembering facts. Those are essential in leadership, but they are not enough. You must assemble them in a way that makes sense before you can make a sound decision or communicate them to your colleagues and the campus community. Your analysis should always be accurate and, when possible, upbeat and positive, in a way that suggests a response which will result in a positive resolution.

ELEVATE THE DISCUSSION. There will be conflicts and disagreements at your university. As you ascribe meaning to those issues, always try to do so in a way that puts the issue into a broader perspective, consistent with the mission and history of the university. When you talk about budget problems, avoid sounding like the budget director, important as that person is to you and the university. Talk about making budget reductions in a way that preserves the core mission, protects tenure, saves money for important initiatives, and shares the burden. That is what leaders do.

FOCUS ON THE ORGANIZATION. Issues at universities too often revolve around whether the president is going to get what he or she wants. Occasionally this is unavoidable, but most of the time it is because of the way the president presented the issue and then responded to an adverse reaction to it. This is not about you; it is about what is best for the university. Occasionally a response to an initiative of yours will be harsh and personal. If your response to the critics is at all like their criticism, you will have sacrificed your job as president and leader and turned it into a fight between two sides. You will then feel compelled to "win" the fight, which you probably will, as you have more authority than your critics. However, you will have paid a price in credibility, made permanent enemies, and made it more difficult for yourself the next time an issue on which you want to move comes along. Also, this type of behavior will make it more difficult to get your decision effectively implemented. Decisions on campus are difficult enough. You do not want a significant number of people on campus hoping it will not succeed. Your responses to criticism should be thoughtful, focused, and measured. It also helps to wait a while to calm down before you respond.

NEVER CONFUSE DISAGREEMENT WITH DISLOYALTY. Under pressure we all have a tendency to think badly of the motives of our critics. Do not act on this natural impulse. People do not see the world they way you do. When appropriate (and it usually is) take the initiative to talk to the people who disagree. You can invite them to your office; but, even better, go to their office, reducing the status distance, and creating more of a conversation between human beings (and probably garnering you a few political points, as well). Vow to listen to what they have to say before you respond. You may understand one another's ideas better, perhaps even learning something yourself. You may also learn about ways to better explain your position. And, perhaps most importantly, you will be interacting as individuals. Never, ever allow yourself to be treated as merely a symbol, "the administration," nor treat another as a symbol, "the faculty."

If a few people are dug in on an issue and simply will not change, it is crucial that you handle those individuals in ways that do not cause them to garner allies. If those few individuals become isolated, one of two things will happen. Ideally, they will want to join the larger group and not remain chronic critics. Failing that, they will remain isolated and will have minimal influence on the rest of the university.

CONSOLIDATE YOUR SUPPORT BEFORE TAKING ON MAJOR INITIATIVES. There are some things that only increase support for your presidency.

Raising money, getting authority to construct a new building, and getting approval for a new degree program are popular. There are also small changes you can make without causing significant opposition on campus and that a majority of the university community can support. The really difficult decisions and initiatives should only be made periodically, ideally when your support is strong, and you have demonstrated your competence and your commitment to the university. Successful presidencies require building a strong base of support and calling on that support when they need to make difficult decisions.

FIND PEOPLE OFF-CAMPUS TO TALK TO. The presidency can be a lonely job. Find a few people to talk to on a regular basis who will listen sympathetically, but not just offer blind support. If you are fortunate, this will include your spouse. There may be another president with whom you have a trusting relationship. University campuses can become very insular places and often it takes someone off campus to put the problem in perspective. In my case, I also tried to periodically treat my job as a consultant would. What would I advise doing if this were my consulting assignment? This permitted me to have some perspective on the issue.

DO NOT TREAT EVERYTHING AS IF IT WERE A MATTER OF PRINCIPLE. If all decisions seem to require that your integrity be on the line, you are raising the stakes too high. When there *are* principles at stake, state them clearly, unemotionally, and understandably. They should not be sacrificed. However, as Steve Sample has written, you must decide what hill you are prepared to die on. There are many shades of gray in administrative life and only periodically are things black and white. You will use yourself up politically, exhaust yourself physically, and make unwise decisions if everything is all-or-nothing, all of the time.

ADMIT MISTAKES. It is difficult to take responsibility occasionally for the mistakes of others, but remind yourself that you will get credit for the good work of others that will more than balance it out. Politicians too often speak in the passive voice: "Mistakes were made." This is not what people want to hear. Organizations do not make mistakes—people do.

When I was a president, the heating system in our residence halls was changed, necessitating the shutting off of heat altogether for several hours. The day chosen was very cold and neither the students nor I were warned that this was going to occur. Not surprisingly, the students were unhappy and complained that the room they had paid for was freezing! I sent an email to the entire campus, explaining what happened, that the idea was sound, but the implementation was terrible, and I apologized. I received an email from a faculty member who had been on the campus for forty years, who said that during his entire time at the college this was the first time a president had apologized or admitted a mistake. I never forgot that lesson.

A SENSE OF PERSPECTIVE. As I wrote this chapter I was tempted to list keeping a sense of humor as one of the ways to avoid failure. Perhaps that should have been mentioned first. Just remember that while you are struggling with a problem that is very difficult and seems all of your own, faculty are meeting with their students in the classrooms and the laboratories. Students are studying, learning about their subjects, about themselves and, on occasion, falling in love with one another. Take a break, talk to someone you trust, think about your problem over the weekend, and try again on Monday morning.

Concluding Thoughts

A Conversation that Never Ends

This book has emphasized the context in which we do our work. I have cited research that convincingly describes how our behavior is affected by the behavior of other people—our community, the organization where we work, and our immediate colleagues. An important part of your job as president is to help create a context in which people can establish trusting relationships to help one another do their jobs and to make their work satisfying and meaningful.

The need for those relationships and that meaning is universal. However, the conditions for establishing and maintaining them are eroding in twenty-first century America. Because of that erosion, the hunger for relationships and meaning is greater because it is often not met in today's society. We should not be surprised that those conditions affect the life of our colleges and universities. The context for university life is the larger society of which we are all a part.

Bart Giamatti, the late president of Yale University, in a commencement address to the graduating class of Franklin and Marshall University, speaking about tensions between and among administrators and faculty on our college campuses, said:

> When administrators believe themselves only managers of the public policy of the place and faculty members believe themselves alone in guarding the flame of intellectual values, when presidents and deans on the one hand and members of the faculty on the other may even question whether they share the same goals, the same mission, the same hopes, then they split apart. They speak of us and THEM. (Giamatti 1990, 44)

The context for our students is in part created and maintained by faculty and administrators at their university. If those students see no difference between how society addresses differences and conflict and how we address our differences on the campus, we have made it easy for them to believe that their college experience consists solely of passing a requisite number of classes, acquiring a requisite number of credits, and getting a well-paying job. If we do that, we will have failed as educators. We may have created skilled workers, but we have not helped shape effective citizens who can contribute to our democracy. Acquiring a liberal education requires examining our beliefs, respecting others, and learning from them about they believe. By not setting an example among our colleagues at our university we provide no alternative model for our students. We let them off the hook. As educators we can only hold our colleagues and students to high standards if we establish and adhere to those standards ourselves. We should never make it easy for our students, or ourselves. We and they deserve better.

You and I know from research, but especially from our own experience, that our students learn as much outside the classroom as inside it. We know that because it was true for us as students. A liberal arts education, surely easier to provide at a small university, offers not only a laboratory for acquiring valuable insights into our past and skills to prepare for the future, it offers a way of thinking about others, ourselves, and how to live our lives. It teaches reason, discipline, logic, and a way of learning from books, in the laboratory, and from one another. This learning involves a conversation.

Leading a university requires initiating and engaging in a continuous conversation. A conversation requires attentiveness, listening, reflecting before responding, and then changing our positions when the evidence convinces us. As president you have a responsibility to create the conditions for that conversation and then to participate in it.

LITERATURE CITED

Allport, Gordon. 1937. The functional autonomy of motives. *American Journal of Psychology* 50:141–156.

Bailyn, Bernard. 2003. *To begin the world anew.* New York: Alfred A. Knopf.

Barber, James David. 1978. *Duke alumni register.* Durham: Duke University.

Birnbaum, Robert. 1988. *How colleges work.* San Francisco: Jossey-Bass.

Birnbaum, Robert. 1992. *How academic leadership works.* San Francisco: Jossey-Bass.

Birnbaum, Robert. 2000. *Management fads in higher education: Where they come from, what they do, why they fail.* San Francisco: Jossey-Bass.

Blau, Peter M. 1960. Structural effects. *American Sociological Review* 25(2):178–193.

Brooks, David. 2000. *Bobos in paradise: The new upper class and how they got there.* New York: Simon & Schuster.

Burns, Tom. 1955. The reference of conduct in small groups: Cliques and cabals in occupational milieux. *Human Relations* 8(4):467–486.

Campion, Michael, David K. Palmer, & James E. Campion. 1997. A review of structure in the interview selection. *Personnel Psychology* 50(3):187–197.

Clark, Burton R. 1970. *The distinctive college: Antioch, Reed, and Swarthmore.* Chicago: Aldine.

Clark, Burton R. 1972. The organizational saga in higher education *Administrative Science Quarterly* 17:178–179.

Cooperman, Alan, & Thomas B. Edsall. 2004. Evangelicals say they led charge for the GOP. *Washington Post*, November 8, Section A:1.

Coover, Robert. 2004. As quoted by Garrison Keillor, *The writer's almanac,* American Public Media (February 4).

de Waal, Franz. 2005. *Our inner ape.* New York: Riverhead Books.

Drucker, Peter. 2001. *The essential Drucker: The best of sixty years of Peter Drucker's essential writings on management.* New York: Harper Collins.

Faulkner, William. 1951. *Requiem for a nun.* New York: Random House.

Fitzgerald, F. Scott. 1936. *Esquire,* February.

Fountain, Henry. 2006. The lonely American just got a bit lonelier. *New York Times, Week in Review,* July 2:12.

Giamatti, A. Bartlett. 1989. *A free and ordered space: The real world of the university.* Gannett Center for Media Studies, 5th Annual Leadership Institute. New York: Gannett Center for Media Studies.

Giamatti, A. Bartlett. 1990. *A free and ordered space: The real world of the university.* New York: W. W. Norton.

Gladwell, Malcolm. 2000a. *The tipping point: How little things can make a big difference.* New York: Little, Brown.

Gladwell, Malcolm. 2000b. The new-boy network. *New Yorker,* May 29: 68–86.

Gladwell, Malcolm. 2002. Political heat: The great Chicago heat wave and other unnatural disasters. *New Yorker,* August 12.

Greenberg, Milton. 2002. An administrator's guide to how faculty members think. *The Chronicle of Higher Education,* March 8:1).

Griffin, John Howard. 1996. *Black like me* (35th anniversary edition). New York: Signet/New American Library.

Handy, Charles. 1994. *The age of paradox.* Cambridge: Harvard Business School Press.

Hesburgh, Theodore M. 1979. *The Hesburgh papers: Higher values in higher education.* Kansas City: Andrews and McMeel.

Jones, Thomas E., Edward V. Stanford, & Goodrich C. White. 1964. *Letters to college presidents.* Englewood Cliffs, NJ: Prentice-Hall.

Jordan, David Starr. 1902. University-building. *Popular Science Monthly* 61(4):330–338.

Kaiser, Robert. 2007. Boss science. *New York Magazine Guides,* April 8:1.

Kanter, Rosabeth Moss. 1989. *When giants learn to dance.* New York: Simon & Schuster.

Keltner, Dachner, & Robert J. Robinson. 1996. Extremism, power and the imagined basis of social conflict. *Current Directions in Psychological Science* 5:101–105.

Kerr, Clark. 2001. *The gold and the blue: A personal memoir of the University of California, 1949–1967.* Berkeley: University of California Press.

Knight, Edgar W. 1940. *What college presidents say.* Chapel Hill: University of North Carolina Press.

Kohr, Steve. 2004. Is Kaiser the future of American health care? *New York Times, Sunday Business,* October 31:4.

Kotter, John P. 1990. *A force for change: How leadership differs from management.* New York: The Free Press.

Kotter, John P. 1999. *What leaders really do*. Cambridge: Harvard Business School Press.

Logan, Ben. 2006. *The land remembers*. Blue Mounds, WI: Itchy Cat Press.

Merton, Robert. 1957. *Social theory and social structure* (revised and enlarged edition). New York: Free Press.

Mickelthwait, John, & Adrian Wooldridge. 1966. *The witch doctors: Making sense of the management gurus*. New York: Random House.

Myers, David G. 2002. *Intuition: Its powers and perils*. New Haven, CT: Yale University Press.

Neustadt, Richard. 1962. *Presidential power*. New York: John Wiley & Sons.

Park, Robert. 1928. Human migration and the marginal man. *The American Journal of Sociology* 33:881–893.

Penson, Edward M. n.d. *Establishing the presidency, establishing the base, the first 500 days*. Tallahassee, FL: Penson Associates Inc.

Penson, Edward M. n.d. *Flashpoints of "troubled" presidencies*. Tallahassee, FL: Penson Associates Inc.

Peterson, Merrill D. 1987. *The Great Triumvirate: Webster, Clay, and Calhoun*. New York: Oxford University Press.

Putnam, Robert. 2006. Fatter, taller and thirstier Americans. *New York Times* December 15:A18.

Putnam, Robert, & Lewis Feldstein. 2003. *Better together: Restoring the American community*. New York: Simon & Schuster.

Rice, R. Eugene, & Ann E. Austin. 1988. High faculty morale: What exemplary colleges do right. *Change* (March/April):52).

Roberts, Sam. 2004. In government we trust (as far as we can throw it). *New York Times*, January 4: 4.

Rosenzweig, Phil. *The halo effect*. New York: The Free Press.

Rubin, Robert, & Jacob Weisberg. 2004. *In an uncertain world: Tough choices from Wall Street to Washington*. New York: Random House.

Sample, Steven B. 2003. *The contrarian's guide to leadership*. San Francisco: Jossey-Bass.

Seymour, Daniel. 1995. *Once upon a campus: Lessons for improving quality and productivity in higher education*. Phoenix, AZ: Oryx Press.

Schuman, Samuel. 2005. *Old Main: Small colleges in the twenty-first century*. Baltimore: Johns Hopkins University Press.

Slosson, Edwin E. 1910. *Great American universities*. New York: MacMillan.

Sunstein, Cass. 2003. *Why societies need dissent*. Cambridge: Harvard University Press.

Surowiecki, James. 2004. *The wisdom of crowds: Why the many are smarter than the few and how collective wisdom shapes business, economics, societies, and nations*. New York: Doubleday.

Thomas, Evan. 2002. The age of sacred terror. *New York Times Book Review*, November 3: 10.

Vazire, Simine, and Funder, David C. 2006. Impulsivity and the self-defeating behavior of narcissists. *Personality and Social Psychology Review* 10(2):154–165.

Veblen, Thorsten. 1918. *The higher learning in America: A memorandum on the conduct of universities by business men.* New York: B. W. Huebsch.

Wills, Gary. 2002. *James Madison.* New York: Macmillan.

Suggested Reading

There are a small group of books that I have found especially useful as a president and a writer. Several of them were released while I served as president; they were helpful in understanding my job and my college. Others I read later, either because I did not get to them while I was president, or they were issued after I retired. I list them here, with short descriptions, and recommend them to you.

Robert Birnbaum. *How Colleges Work.* Jossey-Bass, San Francisco, 1988.

Robert Birnbaum. *How Academic Leadership Works.* Jossey-Bass, San Francisco, 1992.

There are many books on colleges and universities and on academic leadership. These books by Robert Birnbaum are based on careful study and longitudinal research, unlike virtually all of the others. You will recognize your job and your university in them and find them readable as well.

John P. Kotter. *A Force for Change: How Leadership Differs from Management.* The Free Press, New York, 1990.

John P. Kotter. *What Leaders Really Do.* Harvard Business School Press, Cambridge, 1999.

Kotter, Emeritus Professor of Leadership at the Harvard Business School, is one of the best regarded researchers and writers on leadership. These books address important differences between leadership and management, and the behavior of successful executives. While his focus is on business organizations, you will find the information in these books very helpful.

Malcolm Gladwell. *The Tipping Point: How Little Things Can Make a Big Difference.* Little, Brown and Company, New York, 2000.

David G. Myers. *Intuition: Its Powers and Perils.* Yale University Press, New Haven and London, 2002.

These two books, one a bestseller and the other receiving little recognition, are interestingly written and make accessible a great deal of research on individual and group behavior. Be sure to read Chapter 10, "Interviewer Intuition."

Steven B. Sample. *The Contrarian's Guide to Leadership.* Jossey-Bass, San Francisco, 2003.

This book, by the President of the University of Southern California, identifies fifteen important principles of executive leadership. They are summarized in the conclusion. Start reading there. If you find those conclusions interesting—and I am confident you will—go back to the start of the book and read it in its entirety.

Doris Kearns Goodwin. *No Ordinary Time.* Simon and Schuster, New York, 1994.

Doris Kearns Goodwin. *Team of Rivals.* Simon and Schuster, New York, 2005.

The first book by Doris Kearns Goodwin is a detailed account of the lives of Franklin and Eleanor Roosevelt in the White House during WWII. The second book is an account of the men who competed with Abraham Lincoln for the presidency in 1860, his appointment of them to his cabinet, and his leadership during the Civil War.

A glib suggestion would be to say, if you think you have problems as president, read about two men who led our nation through three of its greatest crises, the Civil War, the Great Depression, and WWII. While it may put your struggles as president into a helpful context, these books provide much more than that. They provide insights into leadership, dealing with enormous difficulties and crushing personal burdens, and working with people who do not agree with you. Just as importantly, they will take you away from your job, an important goal from time to time.

INDEX

ABOUT THE AUTHOR

Harry L. Peterson retired as president of Western State College of Colorado in 2002. His administrative career focused on organizational change and external relations.

Earlier in his career he served as an administrator at University of Wisconsin–Green Bay when it opened in 1969 and became a four year university; he reported to three Chancellors at the University of Wisconsin–Madison, including serving as Chief of Staff to Donna Shalala while she was Chancellor at that university. Peterson was Deputy Chancellor of the Minnesota State Colleges and Universities in the mid-1990s, when that system of higher education was created, and Vice President for University Relations and Development at the University of Idaho. He also served in the administrations of two Wisconsin governors.

Peterson received a bachelor's degree from San Diego State University, a master's degree from University of California–Berkeley, postgraduate training at Harvard Medical School and Massachusetts General Hospital, and a Ph.D. from UW–Madison in Education Policy Studies, with an emphasis on organization change. His dissertation was a study of the leadership of Robert Birnbaum at the University of Wisconsin–Oshkosh.

Peterson now consults with college, university, and system presidents, and has conducted presidential evaluations. His clients have included the SUNY–System Administration, SUNY–Fredonia, Holyoke Community College, the

University of Wisconsin System Administration, the University of Wisconsin Colleges, the University of Wisconsin–Madison, and Cedar Crest College. He has served on the Board of Visitors of the School of Education at the University of Wisconsin–Madison, and is a 2004 recipient of the Alumni Achievement Award from that school.

Harry's hobbies include book-collecting and reading—especially biographies, nature studies, and American history. He is an active fly fisher, fly tier, and writer, and has published articles about conservationist Aldo Leopold and fly fishing. He and his wife Sylvia live in Middleton, Wisconsin. He welcomes communication from readers (harrylpeterson@gmail.com).

Reflections on
*Leading a Small College or University:
A Conversation that Never Ends*

There are many helpful books on the college presidency but the perspective and touch of this new contribution is refreshingly human, candid, and accessible. By stressing the experiences of a small college president, this book covers the entire range of direct and immediate encounters with diverse constituencies that might escape the attention of those who lead larger institutions but this comprehensiveness provides a context useful for the presidency of any kind of college and university. It is especially valuable for those who aspire to be a college president, for those who are connected to a college president by governance, and for those who work with and for a college president. In plain language it conveys a real sensitivity to the deep responsibilities and ambiguous controls of the presidency and how that sensitivity is the foundation of effective leadership.

David Ward, President, American Council on Education

This wise manual should be a handbook for all presidents, wannabe presidents, and trustees who hire presidents of small colleges. Its observations and advice spring from the real-life experience of a successful small college president who understands that the special challenges, and rewards, of such leadership differ from those of large university presidencies. It is unique in offering advice about the personal, as well as the professional, challenges presidents face and telling the reader how to recognize when outside expertise is needed and how to use it. Reading this book should enable small college presidents to avoid the big mistakes while gaining the humor and perspective to embrace the wonderful opportunities of this special leadership opportunity.

Moreover, system presidents and boards of trustees who are responsible for hiring college presidents need to appreciate the unique challenges of these positions and muse on how they can help these indispensable leaders succeed in the very special milieu of small colleges and communities.

Katharine Lyall, President-emeritus, University of Wisconsin System

Harry Peterson knows small colleges, their commitment to excellence, their people, their inner dynamics, their quirks and foibles. This manual tells what you need to know —whether you are a sitting or aspiring president, dean, trustee, or citizen dedicated to seeing that small colleges in America remain a primary national resource.

Marvin Henberg, Former Academic Vice President and Interim President,
Linfield College, McMinnville, Oregon

This book belongs on the bookshelf or in the brief case of every small college president or trustee, or anyone who aspires to those posts. Writing in a learned, humane, and genial style, Peterson delivers sage advice based on his personal experience and wide reading on small college leadership. He covers all the bases from the early days of the presidency, to nurturing a leadership team, to board-president relations, and more. His chapter on why otherwise talented people fail as presidents may help save some careers. His focus on the relational aspects of the job—relations with the faculty, students, trustees, and others is especially welcome.

Terry MacTaggart, former Chancellor,
University of Maine System and Minnesota State University System

The only resource better than this handbook for small college presidents would be to know and to work directly with Harry Peterson over a period of time. Lamentably, only a few of us have had that extraordinary privilege and opportunity.

I served as the Vice President for Academic Affairs throughout the six years of Harry's presidency at Western State College of Colorado. The wisdom and insight of his observations about the complexities of small college presidencies come directly from his highly successful career. Our college and the many constituencies that we serve continue to benefit from Harry's insights into communication, organizational management, human interactions and strategic thinking.

I followed Harry as president of our college and his brilliant mentoring has made it possible for me and our campus community to build upon the strong organizational foundation that he established several years ago. *Leading a Small College* is likely the next best thing (though a distant second) to working with Harry.

Jay Helman, President, Western State College of Colorado